Mission-Driven
Business®

Published by Impact Publishing™, Orlando, FL

Impact Publishing™ is a registered trademark.

Printed in the United States of America.

ISBN: 978-0-9961978-8-5
LCCN: 2015948207

This publication is designed to provide accurate and authoritative information with regard to the subject matter covered. It is sold with the understanding that the publisher is not engaged in rendering legal, accounting, or other professional advice. If legal advice or other expert assistance is required, the services of a competent professional should be sought. The opinions expressed by the author in this book are not endorsed by Impact Publishing™ and are the sole responsibility of the author rendering the opinion.

Most Impact Publishing™ titles are available at special quantity discounts for bulk purchases for sales promotions, premiums, fundraising, and educational use. Special versions or book excerpts can also be created to fit specific needs.

For more information, please write:
Impact Publishing™
520 N. Orlando Ave, #2
Winter Park, FL 32789
or call 1.877.261.4930

Mission-Driven Business®

By
Nick Nanton Esq.
and
J.W. Dicks Esq.

Impact Publishing™
Winter Park, Florida

CONTENTS

Foreword 13

BOOK 1
WHY MISSIONS MATTER

CHAPTER 1
THE MAGIC OF MISSIONS 19

CHAPTER 2
**MISSION-DRIVEN
MARKETING POWER** 31

CHAPTER 3
**THE MISSION-DRIVEN
ORGANIZATIONAL ADVANTAGE**....................43

CHAPTER 4
**THE BENEFITS OF MISSION-DRIVEN
BRANDING** 53

CHAPTER 5

**HOW MISSIONS CREATE
INCREDIBLE CHANGE** 65

BOOK 2
YOUR MISSION*:
AN ACTION GUIDE
*(Should you decide to accept it…)

CHAPTER 6

**THE 3-STAGE MISSION-DRIVEN
ACTION PROCESS** 79

ACTION GUIDE STAGE 1:
UNCOVERING YOUR LIFE MISSION 89

CHAPTER 7

FUELING YOUR VEHICLE 99

ACTION GUIDE STAGE 2:
CHOOSING YOUR FUEL AND
DIRECTING YOUR VEHICLE 103

CHAPTER 8

**YOUR ANNUAL CAMPAIGNS
— FROM GOAL TO REALITY** 113

ACTION GUIDE STAGE 3:
FORMULATING YOUR
ANNUAL CAMPAIGNS 119

CHAPTER 9
MARKETING YOUR MISSION 125

CHAPTER 10
**MARKETING YOUR NONPROFIT
MISSION** 135

CHAPTER 11
SAFEGUARDING YOUR MISSION 145

BOOK 3
MISSION MASTERS

CHAPTER 12
THE NONPROFIT MISSION:
Ben Hoyer's Wake-Up Call 161

CHAPTER 13
THE MULTIPLYING MISSION:
Dr. Bill Dorfman's Launching Pad 171

CHAPTER 14

THE GLOBAL MISSION:
Chelsie Antos and the Power
of Sisterhood 181

CHAPTER 15

THE TRANSFORMATIONAL MISSION:
Peter Diamandis' Quest to
Change the World 191

AFTERWORD

NOW, IT'S YOUR TURN 203

FOREWORD

Are you ready to experience "The Phenomenon?"

The Phenomenon is what marketer extraordinaire Dan Kennedy calls the moment in your life when you have the opportunity to make more money in one year than you made in the previous ten. And who's not ready to experience that?

There are many reasons this lucrative window eventually opens up for those of you who consider yourselves entrepreneurs. It could be that years of accumulated learning and business experience have brought you to a place where you instinctively know how to maximize your profits. Or there may be a new breakthrough in technology that you are able to leverage in your own unique way. Perhaps an economic sea change is about to bring a tide of prosperity to your doorstep. Or maybe just plain old good luck will make it happen for you.

Now, all of the above factors can easily create a new level of prosperity for you and your organization – but, as you can see, most of them depend on external circumstances bending in your favor. So, the question becomes, do you really want to wait for the world to deliver The Phenomenon to you - or do you want to create the conditions for it to happen yourself?

And here's the kicker to that latter option – do you want to make the world a better place at the same time?

It may seem like some kind of far-fetched fantasy, but finding massive success through social entrepreneurship actually reflects the reality of today's marketplace. The convergence of new media, disruptive technology and a rethinking from the ground up of what role business should play in today's world has resulted in consumers becoming most receptive to a company that stands for more than just dollars and cents (and in the pages that follow, you'll see the startling statistics that demonstrate this conclusively).

And that's why, today, the Mission-Driven company stands head and shoulders above its competition.

Now you might think the Mission-Driven tag would only apply to 21st century start-ups – relatively new players like Chipotle, with its commitment to quality ingredients, Uber with its revolutionary way of delivering convenient and affordable rides, and Zappos with its sky-high customer service standards.

But the truth is Mission-Driven principles have also brought huge success to such established companies as Federal Express and Newman's Own ever since their founding. More importantly, many other older companies have successfully transformed themselves into Mission-Driven organizations because they saw the necessity of doing so. For example, Dove Soap, a seventy-five-year-old brand, regained its relevance by focusing on women's image issues – and taking the spotlight off its own products! How counter-intuitive is that?

In this book, with the help of Joel Canfield, our talented researcher and writer, you'll be able to discover how all of the above companies and many more found Mission-Driven success – and how you can realize your own. To that end, we'll also provide you with an Action Guide that will help you, your company or even your nonprofit organization uncover a vibrant and rewarding path to prosperity through these principles.

And, by the way, when we say "rewarding," we're not just talking about dollars and cents. And when we say "prosperity," we mean a spiritual wealth as well as a physical one. Part of what's so exciting about being Mission-Driven is that everyone gets something out of it – and for our part, we love engaging in entrepreneurship that benefits others as well as ourselves. Let's face it, the world could use all the help it can get these days - and if business can deliver that help and prosper as a result, that's a great win-win for all concerned.

What does this all mean to you? Well, it means that The Phenomenon can happen not only for you, but for those around you. That's what this book is all about, in our opinion – retooling your organization so that it creates a wave of benefits not only for you but for those you serve.

In conclusion, we hope you enjoy all the work we've poured into this book – but, more importantly, we hope you'll realize how corporate profits and social profits go hand-in-hand in this new age of entrepreneurship, both for start-ups and established organizations.

So get ready to experience your own Phenomenon. Get ready to become Mission-Driven!

BOOK 1
WHY MISSIONS MATTER

*"A man with money is no match against
a man on a mission."*

~ Doyle Brunson

CHAPTER 1

THE MAGIC OF MISSIONS

The Movie Star was not acting like much of a movie star.

It was a week before Christmas and he had the bright idea, after a few beers, to make a giant batch of his special salad dressing recipe in an old bathtub of his basement. The plan was, after it was mixed and completed, he would then pour the dressing into old wine bottles that he would cork and give away as Christmas presents to his neighbors.

But the Movie Star had a problem. He had nothing big enough with which to effectively stir the huge tub of dressing.

He called upon a close friend to help him out. But when the friend arrived, he saw that the Movie Star had found a way to take care of the problem – and the friend was aghast at the solution.

The Movie Star was stirring the giant tub of salad dressing *with a filthy paddle from his canoe* – a canoe that he kept down by the river that ran alongside his house. When the friend objected, the Movie Star offered his theory that somehow the oil and vinegar in the salad counteracted any problems of hygiene that might crop up from his old and disgusting stirring implement.

After the dressing was completed and after all the designated gift bottles were filled, the Movie Star and his friend couldn't believe just how much salad dressing was left over in the tub. That's when the

Movie Star had a great idea…

…why not bottle the rest and sell it through the local stores?

The friend, noting the concoction's unsavory creation, said that was against the law. Rules and regulations for food preparation had to be followed. The Movie Star was undeterred. He enlisted his friend to help him create a real business in which they would sell his salad dressing in supermarkets. The Movie Star would put up the seed money, the friend would do the legwork. Taste and quality would be paramount to the product.

Just as importantly, the profits from the company, should it actually have any, would go exclusively to a mixture of charities – in the words of the Movie Star, "tax-deductible charities and causes, some church-related, others for conservation and ecology and things like that."

From those humble beginnings, the Movie Star, whose name was Paul Newman, launched one of the iconic food brands of our times, Newman's Own. Over the past three decades, it's generated $400 million, all of which was given to countless charities. Today, Newman's Own produces nearly 100 individual food products

No doubt much of its success was due to the quality of the offerings and the celebrity of the company's founder. But, in some cases, celebrity names don't help much! Who remembers Frank Sinatra's neckties? Flavor Flav's fried chicken? Jerry Lewis's movie theatres? Hulk Hogan's Pastamania? Kanye West's women's clothing line?

No, there was a big difference when it came to Newman's own – and the late, great Paul Newman absolutely understood what the real appeal of his Newman's Own line was. He said, "If you can make people aware that things are going to charity, and if there are two competing products on the shelf, maybe people will grab the one where some good will actually come of it."

He understood the power of a mission.

Imagine going to see a James Bond movie where 007 had nothing to do but some paperwork. Consider turning on an episode of a CSI series in which the stars just had coffee and talked about what they had for dinner the previous night. Or think about tackling a video game where the main character had no reason to go anywhere or do anything.

Pretty boring, right? Not to mention pointless and uninteresting. In all of the above cases, if there isn't some kind of mission involved, nobody's going to care and nobody's going to spend time or money on them. Why bother?

Now, think about *your* business - or your non-profit organization.

We're very sure it has a very big mission in *your* eyes – and that's most likely to bring in money. And we have no problem with that. But what we think you should do is take a look at your business from the *public's* eyes. Why should *they* care? What motivates them to buy from it – or, more importantly in terms of developing a vibrant, strong customer, client or donor base - to emotionally engage with it?

That's where having a mission in place can make all the difference.

In our best-selling book, *StorySelling™: Hollywood Secrets Revealed: How to Sell Without Selling by Telling Your Brand Story,* we presented overwhelming evidence that demonstrated the power of storytelling in marketing and branding. In this book, we're going to take that a step further – and show you how to give your organization an incredible ongoing story that will both attract crowds and also keep them at your side for years to come. When you become Mission-Driven, you create a reason to make people root for you – and, even better, do business with you, which they see as a way to support your specific mission. When a business becomes Mission-Driven, it gives itself *a clear and distinct advantage* that its competition lacks. Again, it's all about *StorySelling™* (or selling without selling by telling your brand story) and having a Mission-Driven brand story gives you a narrative that's almost irresistible.

How powerful is having the right mission in a prominent place at your company? So powerful that *it allows you to break every business rule in the book* – and still be incredibly successful.

For example, you can…

- **Give Away Half Your Products**
  Tom's Shoes was a 2006 start-up that announced for every pair of shoes it sold, it would donate a pair of shoes to an impoverished child. After the *Los Angeles Times* ran an article about the new

company, it was suddenly deluged with online orders that accounted for *nine times* its available stock. Toms is currently valued at over $600 million.

- **Tell Customers NOT to Buy from You**
  Could anything be crazier than a company taking out a full-page ad asking its customers NOT to buy what it's selling? That's just what clothing retailer Patagonia did in a full-page *New York Times* ad on Black Friday, 2011 – with a headline that boldly announced, "Don't Buy This Jacket!" They did this in order to announce its "Common Threads" Initiative, promoting sustainability over consumerism. In other words, they wanted people to hang on to their clothing longer and lessen their environmental footprints. That campaign, ironically enough, resulted in the company realizing some of its best sales ever.

- **Stay Closed on the Busiest Day of the Week**
  The national chain Chick-fil-A was founded in 1967 by S. Truett Cathy, who recently passed away at the age of 93. The most unusual thing about these restaurants, has always been that none of them ever open on a Sunday – traditionally a day when many Americans like to eat out. Cathy's reason for that was simple – he was a devout Christian who didn't believe in dealing with money on the "Lord's Day." The company itself states that "Cathy believes that being closed on Sunday says two important things to people: One, that there must be something special about the way Chick-fil-A people view their spiritual life and, two, that there must be something special about how Chick-fil-A feels about its people."[1] Cathy himself said, "I feel it's the best business decision I ever made."[2]

In other words, even though the decision to be closed on Sunday was a genuine belief of Cathy's, he also understood that it sent out a strong signal to customers and employees alike that Chick-fil-A was different than, say, McDonalds or a Burger King. Everything wasn't about making a profit – some things were actually more important to Chick-fil-A. Fast food places are not known for their principles – but Chick-fil-A immediately cut itself apart from that pack by sacrificing at least 14% of its potential revenue for its values.

---

1. Green, Emma, "Chick-fil-A: Selling Chicken With a Side of God," *The Atlantic*, September 8, 2014
2. Ibid

THE CORE COMPONENT OF BEING MISSION-DRIVEN

Being Mission-Driven means you're committed to something above and beyond "business as usual" – even though your mission might be all about business. In our last book, we wrote about how Tony Hsieh (who we've had the privilege to spend some time with along with a few of our top clients in our Mastermind group) built the online shoe retailer Zappos into a billion dollar business – simply by taking customer service to crazy extremes. 99.9% of other business owners would have seen investing such a high amount of time, energy and money in that arena as a waste of resources. And yet, that kind of counter-intuitive move was what made Zappos such a huge sensation. Their mission of gold-plated customer service was exactly what attracted hordes of customers.

The real secret behind Mission-Driven success can be found in the Bible, more specifically in Luke 6:38, which states: *"Give and it will be given to you."* You might make a substantial sacrifice in the short-term – but, long-term, you will make an incredible gain.

And that goes even if you have to commit THE cardinal business sin – and give away your product.

Is there anyone reading this who hasn't heard of TED talks – the famous innovative and engaging 18-minute presentations given by the world's greatest minds? If you haven't heard of them, you're part of a very small group.

The TED conference was first held in 1984 as a one-off event backed by Silicon Valley; it only became an annual event in 1990. Still, you would have been hard-pressed to find many beyond the conference's participants who knew of its existence back then.

That all began to change big-time in June, 2006. That's when TED made their talks available absolutely free for online viewing. Suddenly, the summit that no one had heard of transformed into one of the most successful media organizations in the world.

As Bruno Giussani, the European director of TED, said in 2012, "We started by giving away our content. But for the last three years, we've been giving away our brand, our methods and our formats."[3] It's a concept they call "Radical Openness" – and, as far as they're concerned, no other company or organization in the world has gone as far in opening itself up to the world. What mission drives them?

Giussanni provides the answer. "It's clear to everybody that not only are we living in a globalized world but also an [increasingly complex] world. It's one in which traditional boundaries are breaking down, one after the other. And there are different answers to this. One is that you close. You have protectionism, and borders and tariffs and national preference. And the other is that you open and facilitate additional changes. So we started looking at whether the world is more open or not. And whether it should be more open.

"We found that, giving stuff away, we received even more in return. We have a huge committed community. A lot of brand recognition. And the capacity to touch communities where we had no contact before. The more you open your processes up...the more you receive in return."

For this nonprofit foundation, that last statement rings incredibly true. By 2009, TED talks had been viewed online 50 million times. In 2011, they hit 500 million views. In 2012? They crossed the magic billion mark.

When you bring your beliefs out into the marketplace in a meaningful way, whether you're a nonprofit like TED that wants to create a more intelligent global conversation, or whether you're simply selling shoes like Tom's Shoes or Zappos, it can't help but differentiate yourself from your competition and attract those who are like-minded.

THE 5 PRIMARY ATTRIBUTES
OF A SUCCESSFUL MISSION

With everything in life, there's a catch – and attempting to become successfully Mission-Driven is no different. In this case, how far your mission takes you depends a great deal on (1) what that mission is all about and (2) how you choose to carry it out.

---

3. Cadwalladr, Carole, "TEDGlobal 2012: 'The more you give away the more you get back,'" *The Observer*, June 23, 2012

For example, addressing point 1, if your mission is one that involves strangling kittens, we strongly doubt you'll get much of the public on your side. Conversely, addressing point 2, even if your mission is "pro-kitten," you still will have considerable difficulties if your tactic to help kitties…is to hurt puppies.

You see what we're getting at. You must have in place an admirable purpose – and an admirable way of *fulfilling* that purpose – if your Mission-Driven agenda is really going to have the desirable impact.

With that in mind, we would like to share what we consider to be the 5 Primary Attributes of a Successful Mission. Not all of these have to be in place for a mission to be effective – but each one of them contributes a vital ingredient.

Attribute #1: Positivity
Earlier in this chapter, we discussed how staying closed on Sundays benefited Chick-fil-A's Mission-Driven status. It was a positive for them, as they were giving up potential revenue because of their religious principles – they weren't really hurting anyone besides themselves (and, yeah, okay, also people who wanted a chicken sandwich on a Sunday).

However, when the public discovered Chick-fil-A contributed millions of dollars to groups advocating against same-sex marriage, suddenly the company's mission was seen as polarizing and divisive. True, half of the country flocked to its side, staging "Chick-fil-A Appreciation Days" and spiking their sales during those individual events – but the other half campaigned loudly and vocally against the company, causing many formerly-loyal customers to boycott the chain for good – and even some communities to block new franchises from opening.

The company bounced back when management finally and fully backed away from injecting personal opinion on social issues into their corporate policy. And that's why current CEO Dan Cathy told *USA Today* in 2014, "All of us become more wise as time goes by. We sincerely care about all people." Today, the chain is on track to surpass longtime fast food king McDonalds in overall sales.

The lesson? An organization's mission should always be seen as positive and proactive, and never as punitive or negative. Most of the public does not respond well to that mindset, and the company that employs it risks limiting itself to a small furtive following rather than a broad supportive coalition.

Attribute #2: Relevance

Whatever mission you decide on for your organization should have some meaning to your intended customers, clients or followers. If your mission is to save the sand flea, for example, you probably won't get as much support as you would helping larger social initiatives such as clean water or green energy programs, programs that affect all of us.

Your mission can also be important from a specific service or product standpoint. For example, a food manufacturer who guarantees all its product ingredients are organic or a paper goods company that only uses recyclable ingredients is going to attract customers simply because many of them look for businesses that have these policies in place.

Finally, your mission can be important from the standpoint of your actual business practices. On the About Us page of Southwest Airlines, you'll find their mission very clearly stated: *To connect People to what's important in their lives through friendly, reliable, and low-cost air travel.* Walmart's is even simpler: *Deliver the lowest prices possible.*

To sum up, your mission should not just be relevant to *you*. It's more important that it's relevant to your audience.

Attribute #3: Effectiveness

The name of the decades-long super-successful TV and movie franchise is *Mission: Impossible* – not *Mission: Incompetent.* That concept only works as a comedy. You can have the greatest, most important mission in the world – but if you're perceived to be a failure at that mission, it will hurt you as much as it would have helped you if you had been successful at it.

In 2006, Bono put together an all-star line-up to promote Red, a charitable effort designed to channel money to the Global Fund to Fight AIDS, Tuberculosis and Malaria. Steven Spielberg, Oprah Winfrey, Chris Rock and Christy Turlington were just a few of the superstars enlisted to be public faces of the campaign. Corporate support was also high-profile and mammoth – Gap, Apple and Motorola threw in an estimated $100 million to get the word out.

A year later, all that effort resulted in only about $18 million in donations. Worse, it spurred a backlash against Bono and the companies involved in the campaign, who gave to the fund partly based on how many products they sold through the Red initiative. As Ben Davis, an advertising professional, said in 2007, "The Red campaign proposes consumption as the cure to the world's evils. Can't we just focus on the real solution -- giving money?"[4]

Attribute #4: Altruism

The Red case study reinforces another necessary element to a successful mission – the perception that you're *not just acting in your own best interests.*

Let's return for a moment to the earlier examples of the TED foundation giving away its content and Patagonia telling people not to buy too much of their clothing. In both cases, these organizations are seemingly shooting themselves in the foot – TED, by offering for free its exclusive intellectual property, and Patagonia, by discouraging customers from buying their product. In both cases, however, the public sees companies that *care more about the common good than their own good* – and rewards them for that exemplary behavior.

We all admire the intelligent selfless act – because it seems to happen so rarely. And many of us will then support them for just this reason. In a world where everyone too often seems out to enrich themselves at others' expense, it's refreshing and hopeful to see the opposite behavior in action.

Attribute #5: Engagement

Your mission should also actively cause people to want to be involved with it.

In 2014, the Ice Bucket Challenge took social media by storm – because it was spontaneous (to this date, nobody is sure how it actually started), fun (some of the video bloopers involved were hilarious) and had an altruistic mission (raising money to combat the ALS disease). In just

---

4. Frazier, Mya, "Costly Red Campaign Reaps Meager $18 Million," *Advertising Age*, March 5, 2007

one month, from July 29 to August 29 of 2014, the ALS Association raised $100 million through a simple and virtually-free viral campaign.

Contrast those results with those of the Red campaign we just discussed, where some of the hugest powers-that-be spent countless dollars and time trying to achieve the same effect – and sadly created an extravagant failure (if raising $18 million can rightly be called a failure). In contrast to the Ice Bucket Challenge, Red came across as elitist and mercenary – which, in turn, failed to engage the public at a significant level.

There are many ways that mission engagement can be implemented. The mission could have a direct benefit to a customer (think of Zappos' heightened customer service policies). It could appeal to one's higher instincts (think of Patagonia and TED). Or the organization could simply make it fun to participate (think the Ice Bucket Challenge). We'll discuss engagement in more detail later in this book, but it is one of the most important attributes an organization should have in place. If you can't engage your audience properly, it doesn't really matter how good your mission might be, as Bono discovered to his horror.

If we go back and analyze the mission Paul Newman set out on when he created Newman's Own, we can easily see it had each of the above five attributes in spades.

- *Positivity* – when you saw Newman's smiling face beaming at you from the product packaging, it had to make you feel good about buying.

- *Relevance* – Paul Newman was not only one of the biggest movie stars of his time, he was also one of the most respected, as he was known as someone who used his fame sparingly for only projects he thought mattered. In other words, he was a bit of a Mission-Driven Movie Star! When a guy who wouldn't even sign autographs for fans lent his name to a product line, the public was automatically intrigued.

- *Effectiveness* – his products were well-regarded in terms of quality and taste. More importantly, they quickly earned a lot of money for the charities Newman supported.

- *Altruism* – all after-tax profits went directly to those charities, meaning Newman didn't pocket a cent from his own super-successful company. (We're not saying you have to give all of your profits away, however, this is a clear illustration that happens to be a great example!)

- ***Engagement*** – as noted, the company marketed Newman's involvement in a fun and inviting way. The food itself used as many natural ingredients as possible and the charitable intent was well-publicized. This all added up to create great engagement with consumers.

A Mission-Driven company like Newman's Own can't help but succeed – and it really was ahead of its time. Today, "Cause Marketing" is all the rage and for a good reason: Research shows Mission-Driven companies have huge advantages in today's marketplace.

We'll bring you the facts behind those advantages in our next few chapters.

CHAPTER 2

MISSION-DRIVEN MARKETING POWER

His aunt would bake cookies for him when he was a little boy.

And the cookies were awesome. So awesome that he wanted to make them even...well, awesomer. He always wanted things to be the best they could be and the cookies were no different.

But in the poor neighborhood where he was from, you didn't make it far on cookies. He had to find another way out. He dropped out of high school to join the Air Force. He eventually got his high school equivalency diploma, and, when he was done with his military service, he went to college to learn clerical skills. That, in turn, led to a big break – he got a job as a secretary at the William Morris Agency.

There, his winning personality allowed him to work his way up the ladder, until he became the agency's first African-American talent agent. He also found a great way to attract big clients; he would send them over a batch of his special cookies, made by himself with the killer recipe he developed when he was a boy.

The homemade treats brought him some sweet deals and suddenly, he found himself representing such huge music superstars of the time as Simon & Garfunkel and Diana Ross & the Supremes. And while that was hugely exciting for someone who came from such a humble background, he still couldn't shake the thought that his magical cookies were where his real fortune lay.

So he borrowed seed money from a couple of his multi-millionaire clients, Marvin Gaye and Helen Reddy, and opened his own store in Los Angeles. It was a success. And soon, all of Hollywood was in love with his chocolate cookies.

Hollywood, however, was just one market. He had a leg up there because of his show business connections. The trick was finding a way to market his cookies to the rest of the country.

Instead of hiring an advertising agency to create an expensive campaign that he couldn't afford, the would-be cookie entrepreneur turned to a friend he had recently met who worked at a P.R. firm. That friend, in turn, introduced him to the head of the Literacy Volunteers of America – and the three of them brainstormed a national P.R. tour where the entrepreneur wouldn't sell cookies. No, he would sell *literacy*. It was a cause he passionately believed in because he came from a neighborhood where many never learned how to read and write properly.

Suddenly, his winning personality was being displayed in *People Magazine, Time Magazine*, A&E's "Biography," NBC's "Today Show," ABC's "Good Morning America," *The New York Times, The Chicago Tribune*, plus thousands of daily and weekly newspapers, food trades, and local television stations all across America. Of course, his cookies, which were popping up on supermarket shelves all across America, were mentioned in all these media appearances.

And suddenly those cookies were selling like hotcakes.

Wally "Famous" Amos had become truly famous in one of the very first instances of modern "Cause Marketing" – still used to this day as a textbook example in universities of the power that Mission-Driven marketing can generate above and beyond conventional selling. That power led Famous Amos to sell his brand and company to the Keebler Company in 1998, when Famous Amos Cookies had reached an estimated value of $200 million.

It's been estimated by the Literacy Volunteers of America that Wally Amos brought the problem of illiteracy to the attention of more people than anyone else in history. He didn't just sell cookies – he did a lot of good in spreading an important message.

And yet...many people never remembered the specifics of his mission – just the feeling it gave them. Here's one online blogger who specializes in cause marketing describing how Famous Amos affected him as a kid:

"I remember 'liking' the Famous Amos Company because they were doing something good. I can't remember if I ever tried to convince my parents that by purchasing chocolate chip cookies for me they were doing 'good,' but I certainly should have! ... 'Famous' Amos reminds me of how a brand can associate itself with a cause to the point that it affects the way an individual perceives the brand and its product and can influence purchasing decisions. As if I needed any additional incentive to purchase chocolate chip cookies..."[5]

What a mission can accomplish when it comes to marketing is nothing short of miraculous. The numbers show that the public doesn't just like it when an organization has a specific positive mission, it's starting to see it as a *requirement.*

Here are a few statistics that more than make that case, all taken from the 2013 Cone Communications Social Impact Study:

- 93% of all U.S. consumers say that when a company supports a cause, they have a more positive image (a number that continues to trend up – it was 85% in 2010)
- 91% of global consumers are likely to switch brands in order to support one associated with a good cause
- 90% of Americans are more likely to trust and stay loyal to Mission-Driven companies
- 82% of consumers base buying decisions and what products and services they recommend on a company's support for a cause

Here are a few more dramatic findings:

- 50% of global consumers would be willing to pay more for goods and services if they support companies that give back to society (*Nielsen 2013 Consumers Who Care Study*)

---

5. "Feeling Good about Chocolate Chips," Psgive.org, July 6, 2011, http://blog.psgive.org/post/7308531259/feeling-good-about-chocolate-chip-cookies

- 87% of global consumers believe that business needs to place at least equal weight on society's interests as on business' interests (*2012 Edelman goodpurpose Study*)
- 93% of consumers want to know what companies are doing to make the world a better place and 91% also want to be heard by companies (*2011 Cone/Echo Survey*)

Is it any wonder, with numbers like that, Mission-Driven marketing has always had an edge over the competition?

Yes, being Mission-Driven is truly becoming a requirement for companies. And it's going to become more and more of a requirement in the future, because it's the younger demographics who are driving this kind of dialogue. The Millennials (those born between 1980 and 2000) make up the group which supports cause marketing more than any other – and is the most active in that support. According to the same 2013 Cone Communications Study cited above, Millennials are more apt to use social media to address or engage with companies around social and environmental issues (64% vs. 51% of the general population). 1 in 5 leverages new media to directly support corporate social impact efforts, such as signing pledges and making donations.

But that, of course, doesn't mean you should ignore the Baby Boomer and Senior generations either, when it comes to Mission-Driven Marketing. Boomers still have the most money, spend the most money and are the largest contributors to charities (more than 40% of all money donated comes from Americans aged 49 to 67).[6] And they too are more and more likely to approve of a company that employs cause marketing.

Of course, business notices these kinds of trends, because they can't afford not to. According to a Forbes study in 2011:

- 93% of 311 global executives surveyed believed their company could "create economic value by creating societal value."[7]
- 84% agreed that "companies need to evolve their giving programs from simply giving money to broader social innovation."[8]

6. Blackbaud Inc., "The Next Generation of American Giving," https://www.blackbaud.com/nonprofit-resources/generational-giving-report
7. Forbes Insights, Management and Business Operations, Corporate PhilanthropyThe New Paradigm: Volunteerism. Competence. Results. http://www.forbes.com/forbesinsights/philanthropy_csr_2011/#sthash.zKzMn9ws.dpuf
8. Ibid

The surest sign that Mission-Driven marketing is on the rise? The world's biggest advertising agencies are forming special divisions to address cause marketing. Young & Rubicam, for example, recently created a new "Inspire" group for just this reason. Y&R Chairman and CEO Peter Stringham told *The New York Times,* "It really became apparent there was a need for a mechanism to deliver better than we have been…and proactively line up our resources."

One of the great business legends of our time, Richard Branson, acknowledges this Mission-Driven trend by blogging about what he sees as *"a fundamental transformation taking place in our societies. This transformation is not a technological one – it might be enabled by technology, but it's driven by people and their changing attitudes to participation and change…Here at Virgin we've been using our social media channels to help mobilize support around issues like these… truly understanding what your business can do to make a difference is a critical starting point for any business that wants to thrive in the future.*

And to be open to how your business will need to change in this new world."[9]

THE APPLE OF THE PUBLIC'S EYE

In this chapter's look at Mission-Driven Marketing, we've been dwelling a lot on the heavily-publicized "cause marketing" aspect of a mission – pro-social and frequently charitable endeavors with which businesses align themselves, as Famous Amos did, to create a halo effect around their operation.

But, as we made clear in the first chapter, your mission doesn't have to be limited to that category. It can simply be about the way you do business – and it can still connect with the public with the same power.

Now, there have been millions of pages written over the years about the genius of Steve Jobs and Apple, but rarely within the context we're going to employ here: As an individual, he was completely Mission-Driven. That Mission became an essential part of his personal brand and Apple's corporate brand when he was at the helm; it was the motivating factor behind all his products.

---

9. Branson, Richard. "Occupy Yourself." January 22, 2014, http://www.virgin.com/richard-branson/occupy-yourself

In 2011, when he introduced the iPad2, he made this statement: *"It is in Apple's DNA that technology alone is not enough - it's technology married with liberal arts, married with the humanities, that yields us the results that make our heart sing."*[10]

Now, can you imagine Bill Gates saying something like that? Or most CEOs for that matter?

Because Jobs himself stood for more than just technology, because he made Apple adhere to incredibly high goals for usability and style when it came to all of its products, he set a new standard for a Mission-Driven business that he made sure extended to Apple's marketing. Here's another quote from Jobs that defines the necessity of Mission-Driven Marketing – and the incredible power of it:

"Marketing is about values. It's a complicated and noisy world, and we're not going to get a chance to get people to remember much about us. No company is. So we have to be really clear about what we want them to know about us."[11]

He also constantly asked two questions when it came to the company's marketing:

Question #1: Who is Apple?

Question #2: What does Apple stand for and where do we fit in this world?

His answer to those questions – and, ultimately, Apple's mission: *"Apple believes that people with passion can change the world for the better. And those people that are crazy enough to think that they can, are the ones who actually do."*[12]

Now, keep those words in mind, as we present the copy from one of the most famous Apple ad campaigns of all time, 1997's "Think Different":

"Here's to the crazy ones. The misfits. The rebels. The troublemakers. The round pegs in the square holes.

10. Lehrer, Jonah. "Steve Jobs: "Technology Alone Is Not Enough," *The New Yorker*, October 7, 2011

11. Byerlee, Dana. "What Steve Jobs Knew About the Importance of Values to Your Company," *Yahoo! Small Business Advisor*, Tuesday, August 6 https://smallbusiness.yahoo.com/advisor/steve-jobs-knew-importance-values-company-235014359.html

12. Ibid

The ones who see things differently. They're not fond of rules. And they have no respect for the status quo. You can quote them, disagree with them, glorify or vilify them.

But the only thing you can't do is ignore them. Because they change things. They invent. They imagine. They heal. They explore. They create. They inspire. They push the human race forward.

Maybe they have to be crazy.

How else can you stare at an empty canvas and see a work of art? Or sit in silence and hear a song that's never been written? Or gaze at a red planet and see a laboratory on wheels?

We make tools for these kinds of people.

While some see them as the crazy ones, we see genius. Because the people who are crazy enough to think they can change the world, are the ones who do."

Few can do Mission-Driven like Steve Jobs did. And the pay-off for how well he marketed that Mission?

- Apple has won the CMO Survey Award for Marketing Excellence (chosen by the world's top marketers) for 6 years straight.
- Apple was voted the most Powerful Brand in the World in 2012 in a *Forbes* study.[13]

MASTERING MISSION-DRIVEN MARKETING

When you want to learn how to do something, you turn to the best for inspiration. In this case, Apple is undeniably the master – so let's close out this chapter with some "Apple Axioms" that illustrate the most important Mission-Driven marketing lessons we've learned from this icon for the ages.

Apple Axiom #1: Stand for something or stand for nothing.
If you check out the online website, UrbanDictionary.com, you'll find one of the terms listed is "Apple Hater," whose definition reads in part, "Apple haters dislike the success of the

---

13. Koprowski, Evon. "Apple Is the Most Powerful Brand in the World, According to New Forbes Study," Storyism.net, October 12, 2012 http://storyism.net/apple-is-the-most-power-ful-brand-in-the-world-according-to-new-forbes-study

company and attempt to undermine consumers." Yes, because Apple's success has created a furtive and epically huge band of followers, there had to be a backlash. Whenever a company like Apple, a company with a firm, fixed identity and, yes, mission, stands out from the herd, there will be those who hate it just so *they* can also stand out from the herd.

As long as your mission has the right combination of attributes (which we discussed in the first chapter), you shouldn't concern yourself if your marketing happens to alienate a small portion of your potential customer or client base. It's inevitable – and it also makes your mission seem that much more authentic in the eyes of the public. You're not afraid to lose a few customers that don't believe in your mission. As long as you're positive and pro-active, never defensive and angry, small pockets of protest won't make the smallest dent in your brand.

Apple Axiom #2: Your people must represent Your Mission.
If you've ever been to an Apple Store, you know that the personnel is selling the Apple company culture just as much as its individual products. That's because Apple is careful to make sure their employees fully *understand and represent their mission.* In the words of one, "Sometimes the company can feel like a cult. Like, they give us all this little paper pamphlet, and it says things like—and I'm paraphrasing here—'Apple is our soul, our people are our soul.' Or 'We aim to provide technological greatness.'"[14]

Your marketing isn't just about selling your mission to your potential customers, it's also about selling your mission to your employees and representatives – even, in some cases, your vendors. Zappos is another company that takes this principle very seriously, being so careful to make sure their employees fully support their company culture that, in the past, they've offered them money to quit!

Apple Axiom #3: Keep things simple.
Is there anything simpler – or more iconic – than the Apple logo itself? And is there anything more brilliant than including a sticker of that logo in every iPhone box?

Apple's actual mission is a fairly complex one – and yet the company

---

14. Anonymous, "Confessions of an Apple Store Employee," *Popular Mechanics,* December 21, 2012

is brilliant at communicating its essential essence with incredibly basic messaging. How basic? How about introducing such seminal products as the original Macintosh computer, the iMac and the iPod with just one word – "Hello."

Okay, they got a little wordier with the iPhone – those ads used the tagline, "Say hello to iPhone."

You might ask, well, what does saying "Hello" actually have to do with Apple's Mission? Plenty. Each new Apple product has a certain distinct "cool" look that immediately reflects the company's mandate to continually create beautiful new gadgets that deliver as much cutting-edge style as technology. Simply *showing* one of their new products with a friendly greeting says to the average consumer, "We did it again!"

Or, in other words, Mission Accomplished.

Apple Axiom #4: Influence the Influencers.
In order to introduce the first Macintosh personal computer, Apple aired a special commercial nationally *only one time* – during the 1984 Super Bowl. And this was no quickie; it was directed by a major movie director, Ridley Scott (*"Alien," "Blade Runner," "Gladiator,"* etc.) at the then-unheard-of price of $900,000. "1984," which was the title of the ad, ended up in the Clio Hall of Fame and was named to *Advertising Age*'s 50 greatest commercials of all time.

But before all that happened, just after the commercial was completed and before it aired, it was screened for the Apple Board of Directors. They *hated* it. As a matter of fact, they never wanted it to see the light of day. Jobs insisted, the spot ran for its single airing during the Super Bowl, and the rest is history.

The commercial was more than an advertisement for the Macintosh itself – it was designed to create a conversation about the transformation of society through PCs. As Brent Thomas, the art director of "1984" said at the time, Apple "had wanted something to stop America in its tracks, to make people think about computers, to make them think about Macintosh…This was strictly a marketing position."[15]

15. Burnham, David. "The Computer, the Consumer and Privacy." *The New York Times*, March 4, 1984

Apple's marketing has always been as much about reaching the intelligentsia as its customer base. By aiming at influencing the influencers, their marketing achieves a high degree of credibility and prestige that goes beyond the usual retail selling. "1984" made everybody talk about Apple, even though the ad itself disappeared forever (well, you can still watch it on YouTube). It's "once-and-done" nature just made it all the more compelling.

You also want your organization's mission to be understood and respected by those in a position to validate and amplify your marketing message. Third party validation is always an incredible positive for any marketing campaign. The more "buzz" you can create for your mission, the more you impact the general culture.

Apple Axiom #5: Avoid conflict between your marketing and your Mission.
Anyone who studies marketing remembers the "1984" commercial. But very few talk about its follow-up.

In 1985, Apple presented another "event" commercial for the Super Bowl, designed to capitalize on the massive impact they had made the year before. Apple actually placed full page ads in newspapers around the country, telling readers to make sure and watch during the third quarter for their new sensational commercial – and gave special cushy seats and signs to everybody in the stadium at the actual Super Bowl.

All of this ballyhoo resulted in one of the company's biggest marketing failures. This commercial was received so poorly, Apple didn't place another ad in the Super Bowl for another 14 years!

The ad was called "Lemmings," and its purpose was to introduce Apple's new Macintosh Office software. It did this by portraying hundreds of blindfolded businessmen and women walking off a cliff to their doom – insinuating that everybody was using a PC instead of a Mac was, basically, a self-destructive sheep. Problem was, many more people fit into the former category rather than the latter. As one journalist put it, "Turns out that insulting the very people you are trying to sell merchandise to is not the best idea."[16]

16. Seibold, Chris. "January 20, 1985: Apple Goes to the Well One Too Many Times." AppleMatters.com, January 20, 2011. http://www.applematters.com/article/january-20-1985-apple-goes-to-the-well-one-too-many-times/

"1984" dramatized someone changing the status quo in an exciting and vivid way; "Lemmings" dramatized hordes of people willingly walking into an abyss to die. One vision was stimulating – the other was just plain depressing.

Apple's mission, up until then, had been to *inspire* new ways of thinking and doing – "Lemmings," in contrast, was more of a scare tactic to motivate people into buying Apple products. It was a rare misstep by THE master marketer – and it demonstrated the necessity of keeping the spirit of whatever your Mission might be in whatever marketing you're currently planning.

The melding of mission and marketing is an incredible plus for any entrepreneur, business or nonprofit organization. It reinforces all the benefits that your Mission brings to the table, while elevating your marketing above the crowd with a subtext that stands out.

Being Mission-Driven also provides many verifiable and practical benefits to the internal operation of your organization. We'll look more closely at those benefits in the next chapter.

CHAPTER 3

THE MISSION-DRIVEN ORGANIZATIONAL ADVANTAGE

After 26 years of imprisonment in various jails, the South African authorities were finally going to release the legendary leader Nelson Mandela from prison. It was 1990 – and, the age of apartheid, the policy that had divided a nation and spurred Mandela to revolution, was finally over. There was excitement in the air and a celebratory mood in the country's black communities.

Just prior to Mandela's release, however, a new general manager arrived in the country to assume control of the troubled Mercedes Benz factory located in the Cape Province port of East London. A militant union, one of the first black unions to be recognized in the country, had created many work stoppages due to distrust of management - and quality control issues were also a continual headache.

The new general manager was already anxious about how he could motivate his workers to improve their job performance, when he was immediately hit with a demand from them. The union was also ecstatic about Mandela's release and wanted to do something special for him – so it requested permission to build Mandela a special Mercedes that could be presented to him on the day he was finally freed from prison.

What many employers might have seen as another impractical demand from a stubborn union was instead seen as a golden opportunity by the new general manager to create a new bond between management and workers. He went ahead and took the request to his superiors. He needed a fast answer, as it was Monday and Mandela was due to be released that weekend.

Fortunately, upper management quickly said yes – and also agreed to provide special car parts for the job. For their part, the union workers agreed to build the car during unpaid overtime hours, so the factory's output wouldn't be diminished.

Galvanized by their new goal, the factory workers labored day and night. They set aside a special block on the factory which they tagged as Mandela's car and danced and sang as they worked on it on their own time. They finished the vehicle in a record four days, just in time. Mandela was delighted to receive this unexpected gift, a new red top-of-the-line S500, which came to be known as "Madiba's Merc" (Madiba being Mandela's clan name).

Quality and productivity numbers went up at the plant after that unifying mission tied the workers to each other and to the company management. Eight years later, in 1998, the chairman of the Daimler Chrysler AG group, which owned the Benz brand, decided to invest a whopping one billion dollars into the thriving East London plant. On the day he announced this epic plant expansion, by his side stood none other than Nelson Mandela, grinning from ear to ear.

The assembling of "Madiba's Merc" was a pivotal moment for the country of South Africa. The evidence of that is the fact that the car, which featured an inscribed South African flag and Mandela's name, can now be seen on display at the Apartheid Museum in Johannesburg. But it was just as pivotal for the South African Mercedes Benz operation, because it made the company an established force in the new post-apartheid regime.

Why? Because the carmaker took on a mission that transformed its workforce from an angry recalcitrant bunch of workers to a unified group that felt supported and energized by a management.

Many financial experts find it easy to take potshots at a company that applies itself to a mission that doesn't seem to have a direct impact on the bottom line. But, as the Mercedes-Benz South Africa story above demonstrates, the right mission can bring to life amazing results in almost every aspect of the organization, both inside and out – as well as continue to deliver ongoing benefits that grow and grow.

Unfortunately, the accountants of the world tend to tune out when companies begin taking on big (and sometimes expensive) missions – they don't see the real dollars-and-cents benefits to the bottom line. Well, this is the chapter you need to show them if you're getting that kind of blowback – because, in the next few pages, we're going to take a closer look at the distinct and powerful *business* advantages of having a mission in place.

HOW MISSIONS POWER UP YOUR OPERATION

Philipp Groom, an employee of the South African Mercedes Benz company, made a short film about the creation of the special Mandela Mercedes and had this to say about it: "All workers wanted to be part of this, they wanted to touch this vehicle."[17]

Now, allowing these employees to build the car didn't cost this huge company a whole lot – but, as we noted, it ended up benefiting the company in many powerful ways. Perhaps the most important benefit was that it bolstered *employee engagement.*

If you're unfamiliar with the concept of employee engagement, it's time you got up to speed. Because whether you're running a huge corporation or you're an entrepreneur with a minimal office staff of 3 or 4, employee engagement happens to be a huge deal when it comes to optimizing the internal operation of your company.

How huge a deal? That's actually easy to ascertain, because employee engagement has been one of the most researched business issues in recent years. And the results of those studies show that high engagement invariably shows up as a big business plus.

Here are a couple of the most significant benefits, according to Gallup's most recent *State of the American Workplace* report, which studied companies over a two-year period:

---

17. Davies, Alex. "South African Mercedes-Benz Workers Made This Car For Nelson Mandela When He Was Released From Prison." Business Insider, December 6, 2013. http://www. businessinsider.com/nelson-mandela-mercedes-benz-south-africa-2013-12

- **Engaged workers are the lifeblood of their organizations.**

The **top 25% of engaged companies** Gallup studied have significantly higher productivity, profitability, and customer ratings, less turnover and absenteeism, and fewer safety incidents than those in the bottom 25%.

Those businesses with more engaged workers also experienced **147% higher earnings per share (EPS)** compared with their competition in 2011-2012. On the other hand, active disengagement costs the U.S. *$450 billion to $550 billion per year.*

- **Engagement drives higher performance more than any company policies or perks.**

Engaged employees work hard and are more likely to put in extra hours. Engagement also has **a higher impact** on an employee's well-being than any company benefits.

Gallup isn't alone with their engagement conclusions. Accenture, the world's largest consulting firm, also found through their research that:

- **Less than 50% of CFOs** understand the enormous ROI (Return on Investment) when it comes to funding initiatives designed to increase employee engagement.

- Organizations that invested just another 10% into engagement initiatives would increase profits by *$2400 per employee*.

So what do missions have to do with employee engagement, you might be asking by now. Don't people just want more money? Isn't that all you need to do to increase engagement?

Well, that's always the go-to answer, but it turns out not to be true. Engagement does *not* result simply from increasing salaries – although nobody believes that! The truth is **89%** of employers believe workers leave to make more money, when in reality...

...only **12%** of employees leave for that reason!!!

There's no question that people appreciate being paid at a fair rate and that does contribute to a certain satisfaction level. BUT...positive engagement actually *trumps money* in most employees' minds – and that's a fact most business people are completely oblivious about.

So yes, you want to have employee engagement in your organization. But the next question is – how do you get it? What's the biggest proven driver of employee engagement?

Well, according to research generated by the Hay Group, a global management consulting firm with 87 offices in 49 countries as of 2013, it's *"Inspiration and Values."* And where do inspiration and values spring from? From our experience, they're both generated directly by a company's mission. The right mission is what it took to create those attributes for the South African Mercedes workers – and your workers will be no different.

Of course, Inspiration and Values don't do the job alone. But research also shows that, without them, none of the other employee engagement drivers do the job at all! Although the Hay Group named a total 6 elements necessary to engagement[18], they found that "Inspiration and Values" was the most critical component. In their words: *"In its absence, delivering on the other five elements of the Engaged Performance model is unlikely to engage employees."*[19]

Here's more detail on how being Mission-Driven impacts engagement and the bottom line, from Gallup, the preeminent researcher of employee engagement:

"In conducting a meta-analysis of 49,928 business units across 192 organizations representing 49 different industries in 34 countries, Gallup scientists discovered that margin and mission are not at odds with one another at all. In fact, the opposite is true. As employees move beyond the basics of employee engagement and view their contribution to the organization more broadly, they are more likely to stay, take proactive steps to create a safe environment, have higher productivity, and connect with customers to the benefit of the organization."[20]

All good, right?

---

18. Other 5 Elements of Employee Engagement named by the Hay Group are (1) Quality of Work, (2) Tangible Rewards, (3) Work/Life Balance, (4) Enabling Environment, (5) Future Growth/Opportunity

19. Engage Employees and Boost Performance, Hay Group Working Paper, http://www.hay-group.com/downloads/us/engaged_performance_120401.pdf

20. Groscurth, Chris. "Why Your Company Must Be Mission-Driven." Gallup Business Journal, March 6, 2014. http://www.gallup.com/businessjournal/167633/why-company-mission-driven.aspx

The mammoth impact of a galvanizing mission on even the lowest-ranked employee is best illustrated by what is perhaps an apocryphal anecdote, but nevertheless, a revealing one. Supposedly, in the 60's, a janitor at NASA was asked what he was doing. His reply? "Helping to put a man on the moon."

And by the way, missions don't just help workers do their jobs better – if you're running your own business or in a management position, missions also help YOU do your job better.

Deloitte is a national business consulting firm with 65,000 employees – and they too have studied how missions positively affect organizations. One of the most important ways missions do that is by giving business leaders *confidence*. A couple more statistics from their study:

- **82 percent** of leaders whose companies have a strong sense of purpose expected to grow in 2014, compared to **just 67 percent** of leaders who didn't feel Mission-Driven

- **91 percent** of leaders at Mission-Driven companies felt their companies would strengthen or maintain their brand in the next 5-10 years, compared to **just 49 percent** of other owners/managers[21]

Most of you reading this book are aware of the power of positive thinking: if you believe it, you can usually do it. Conversely, if you lack that kind of confidence, you more frequently fail.

Missions can be invaluable in providing that kind of confidence. When your company is Mission-Driven, you are working towards a purpose you truly believe in and commit to – you, in effect, have a road map in place that you can follow to take your business to your desired destination. Without that mission? Well, you're engaged in only a day-to-day grind, with no ultimate aim in mind (except perhaps to earn a profit). It's hard to feel confident when you have no real direction in what you're doing.

To be Zen about it, if you don't know where you're going, how can you get there?

---

21. Vacarro, Adam. "How a Sense of Purpose Boosts Engagement," *Inc. Magazine*, April 18th, 2014.

THE 5 BIGGEST BUSINESS BENEFITS
OF BEING MISSION-DRIVEN

It's easy to see how an organization without a mission can end up as an organization that seems to lack leadership. Just look at the situation through your own viewpoint; when, as an individual, you feel you have purpose and something driving you forward in your life and/or work, we're willing to bet you feel more excited, more directed and better able to realize meaningful results. But when you don't.... you probably feel a little lost, unmotivated and maybe even unproductive.

A business is no different. A mission declares the difference it wants to make in the world and what it stands for. Again, whether that mission is a pro-social charitable one or one that involves a unique way the company approaches its products and services, it still creates a definition that hopefully connects both with the external public and your internal workforce.

As we mentioned earlier, the Gallup research company has done an incredible amount of research on what makes businesses succeed – and they've identified 5 specific ways that being Mission-Driven promotes success and profits in any business.[22]

1. **Mission-Driven companies inspire loyalty in employees of all ages.**
   As noted, employees aren't just driven by money – they also want to feel like they can answer the question, "Do I belong here?" with a resounding "Yes!" According to Gallup, that means, in addition to providing opportunities for them to do what they do best, mission and purpose have to be emphasized as much as possible. That's the key to employee retention and performance. Without those Mission-Driven elements in place, you can easily lose valuable employees if they're offered a comparable salary and/or position from someone else.

   Think about the janitor from NASA – he's never going to take a job anywhere else. After all, where else can a person work and help get people to the moon?

---

22. Groscurth

49

2. A mission creates customer engagement.

The right mission not only engages management and workers alike, it also helps a company connect to its customers. As we noted in the last chapter, one of the biggest examples of that is Apple. Its customers know that that company's newest product is always going to be revolutionary in some way – even the smallest iPhone upgrade contains new and exciting surprises.

When a customer knows what to expect from a company's mission – and, more importantly, can rely on them following through on that mission – they're more inclined to return to buy more over the years.

3. A mission creates clarity.

A mission provides a company with a basic understanding of who it is and what it's supposed to be doing. When those big issues are settled, everyone is suddenly on the same page as far as what the company's philosophy is and what needs to be achieved. That can't help but create a unifying clarity that inspires dedication and conviction.

4. A mission optimizes strategic alignment.

The above-mentioned clarity, once set in stone, then permeates an entire organization, allowing it to achieve an overall structural integrity. When addressing operational details, it just becomes a matter of filling in the blanks – and determining what serves the mission (as well as eliminating everything that doesn't).

Take Zappo's commitment to customer service. Once that mission had been decided upon, the Zappos management and workers knew they had to do all they could at every level to make customer service a recognizable priority. It was only a question of defining how far they wanted to take that mission and how to find the right employees who could deliver on it. Everyone knew what the big picture was, so it only became a matter of coloring inside the lines at every level.

5. Missions can be measured.

Because a mission can't help but create strict definitions for your business, it also provides specific benchmarks from which to set goals beyond the usual profit targets. This allows a company to measure how real its intended culture has become and how well it's carrying out its intended mission.

Two important ways to do that is to survey both your customers and your employees. In the case of the latter, you need to make sure your employees both understand your mission and on how best to deliver on it in their specific positions. In the case of the former, it's crucial to research how well your mission is being identified by your customers/clients and how well they think it is being carried out. Imagine if nobody had noticed Zappos' customer service mission – or Apple's commitment to superior style and technology. Both those companies would have quickly retreated and rebooted to find ways to successfully implement their mandates, thereby saving them from getting lost in the shuffle with other similar businesses.

When it comes to getting the nuts and bolts of your business operation just right…when it comes to inspiring both your own people as well as your customers…when it comes to keeping an organization on the same specific track…nothing beats a mission. All available research confirms the very real and very lasting business advantages for any company that chooses to commit to one.

In the next chapter, we'll go further in-depth on one very big and very potent advantage a mission brings any business: branding. Branding, of course, is very much about establishing an identity in the public's mind – and a mission is one of the very best ways to not only create an identity, but make it a living, breathing thing for everyone involved.

CHAPTER 4

THE BENEFITS OF MISSION-DRIVEN BRANDING

They were best friends since they were kids, born only four days apart. But adulthood had proven to be something of a rocky road for both of them.

The one had tried a couple different colleges, but ended up dropping out of them. He wasn't the most motivated student and found himself teaching a pottery class instead. The other one? He made it through college, but found his dreams of becoming a doctor dashed when he couldn't get accepted into medical school.

Both of them were at a dead end with their lives and they were only in their twenties. They talked and decided to try starting a business together. Maybe a food business, since they both had been kind of chunky kids who, ironically, had met in gym class. Still, making food would be a big challenge for at least one of them, who had a sinus condition known as anosmia. That made it extremely difficult for him to smell or even taste anything!

At first, they thought about making bagels – they had loved them growing up on Long Island. But even buying a used bagel-making machine was too expensive. Ice cream? Now *that* was doable. So they took a $5 Penn State correspondence class on ice cream making and then invested all the money they had, $12,000, so they could open a small shop in New England. Even though it was in a cold climate, they had found a college town without an ice cream shop – and saw that as an opportunity.

What ended up making their ice cream stand out? A weakness that inadvertently became a strength. The one partner's sinus condition caused him to demand stronger flavors in their ice cream recipes, so he could actually get some taste out of their own product. The other partner argued against it, saying it would be too much, but it wasn't. Their unusually powerful ice cream concoctions clicked with the college crowd.

The store became instantly successful. On the first anniversary of its opening, the owners held a "Free Cone Day," where they gave away a free ice cream cone to every customer. That and a yearly film festival they sponsored helped make them a vital part of the community. Their local support mushroomed.

But money was still a huge problem – in the winter, there was more of it going out than coming in. They began to study brochures put out by the Small Business Administration that cost 20 cents apiece at the Post Office. They franchised a couple other stores in the region. They began selling pints of their ice cream flavors to local stores. And finally, they began to see some real money coming in.

That's when they began some soul-searching. These two guys had been almost-hippies who had grown up in the 60's, so they wanted their business to represent that spirit. They wanted to put their social mission at the center of everything they did. They wanted to always have what they called "the double dip" in place – profits *and* people.

They started with their own people. They put in place a policy that no employee's rate of pay would be greater than five times that of entry-level employees. In 1995, that meant entry-level employees were paid $12 hourly and the CEO could only be paid $150,000 annually.

Then they moved on to the world at large. At the end of each month, the two of them would ask of themselves and the company, how much had they improved the quality of life in the community?

As the company's need for capital increased, they resisted venture capitalist financing, which typically requires relinquishing significant control over the company. Instead, it sold stock to residents in the region, keeping the company in local hands. In 1985, it officially created a foundation, to which the company would contribute 7.5 percent of its pretax profits.

They also made social activism a critical aspect of their operations, putting into action such projects as:

- An original scoop shop made of recycled materials
- Creation of a "Green Team" in 1989, focusing on environmental education throughout the company
- A company bus equipped with solar panels
- The use of hormone-free milk in its products
- A commitment to reducing solid and dairy waste, recycling, and water and energy conservation at the company's facilities

Ben Cohen and Jerry Greenfield's Ben & Jerry's ice cream brand ended up with annual sales of over $250 million by the end of the 90's – and was sold to Unilever for over $325 million in 2000. Today, it's regarded as the top premium ice cream brand in the world – and, even though it's now owned by a giant corporation, it still continues its "mission" to this day.

Actually, it has *three* missions, which you can find on their current website:

Our Product Mission drives us to make fantastic ice cream – for its own sake.

To make, distribute and sell the finest quality all natural ice cream and euphoric concoctions with a continued commitment to incorporating wholesome, natural ingredients and promoting business practices that respect the Earth and the Environment.

Our Economic Mission asks us to manage our Company for sustainable financial growth.

To operate the Company on a sustainable financial basis of profitable growth, increasing value for our stakeholders and expanding opportunities for development and career growth for our employees.

Our Social Mission compels us to use our Company in innovative ways to make the world a better place.

To operate the company in a way that actively recognizes the central role that business plays in society by initiating innovative ways to improve the quality of life locally, nationally and internationally."[23]

Three missions, one big success. But still, we have to ask the question, how did two broke unemployed hippies reach such rarified business heights?

No doubt such iconic flavors as Cherry Garcia and Chunky Monkey helped propel them to the top – but, just as importantly, it was also the company's bigger societal mission that encouraged people to both invest in them and buy their ice cream. A 1995 article put it this way:

"As the stockholders made clear, their investment in this ice cream company has less to do with its profitability than how it goes about making its profits. What Ben & Jerry's offers its investors is the chance to buy into a company that reminds them of themselves. A company that is innovative and impassioned about its product, but also values-driven. A company with a free-wheeling sense of humor, but also a serious commitment to its community. Business on a human scale, in other words..."[24]

Or, as co-founder Jerry Greenfield himself said, revealing the real secret of their brand:

"...we knew that's what would separate Ben & Jerry's — even more than the great flavors, it was important for us to make our social mission a central part of the company."[25]

As the Ben and Jerry's story demonstrates, a mission can create a powerful and lasting brand that can continue to draw customers, grow profits and do good things for the world all at the same time.

---

23. http://www.benjerry.com/values
24. Carlin, Peter. "Pure Profit: For Small Companies That Stress Social Values as Much as the Bottom Line, Growing Up Hasn't Been an Easy Task. Just Ask Ben & Jerry's, Patagonia and Starbucks." *The Los Angeles Times*, February 5, 1995.
25. Harrison, J.D. "When We Were Small: Ben & Jerry's."
    The Washington Post, May 14, 2014.

Without that mission, however…?

Well, Unilever, the multinational conglomerate that bought the company in 2000, found out the answer to that question. After Ben and Jerry sold the business, the brand went into a slump because, first of all, the brand's true believers thought the founders had also sold out the company's mission – and second of all, that turned out to be largely true. Unilever effectively shut the founders out of any decision-making and also curtailed the do-gooder missions of the company. To them, all that stuff was just some kind of marketing ploy (see chapter 2!).

That's why, in 2004, when Walt Freese was named as Unilever's CEO, he quickly invited Ben and Jerry back into the fold to reinvigorate the company's mission – and, of course, the brand itself. Once that mission was again completely back on track, so was the company. How important is that mission to this day?

Well, in 2010, Jostein Solheim, a Unilever executive from Norway, became the new CEO of the company and had this to say about the transition:

"The world needs dramatic change to address the social and environmental challenges we are facing. Values-led businesses can play a critical role in driving that positive change. We need to lead by example, and prove to the world that this is the best way to run a business. Historically, this company has been and must continue to be a pioneer to continually challenge how business can be a force for good and address inequities inherent in global business." [26]

In other words, in the case of Ben & Jerry's, the mission and the business were inseparable. Each made the other all the more powerful.

MISSION-DRIVEN BRANDING:
THE NEW PARADIGM

It used to be enough to make customers *feel* something.

It was "the Age of Emotion" for branding. In the words of *Advertising Age*, *"Prompted by booms of products and prosperity, conspicuous consumption kicked into high gear, and logic wasn't enough. Your*

---

26. "Division President: Jostein Solheim, Ben & Jerry's Homemade," FoodProcessing.com, http://www.foodprocessing.com/ceo/jostein-solheim/

product had to make a prospective buyer feel something. A car was freedom on four wheels, jeans made you rebellious."[27]

Yes, branding used to be all about tugging the heartstrings. For example, back in the 1970's, the classic heartwarming Coke commercial featuring football player "Mean" Joe Greene throwing a kid his jersey would make a nation sigh and open another bottle of Coke. McDonalds' famous song-and-dance "You Deserve a Break Today" campaign would motivate families to give Mom the night off from cooking and go get some Big Macs, while Kodak would sell its cameras and film with sentimental family photos and a goopy Paul Anka jingle, "For the Times of Your Life."

Today? Because you can instantly take photos with your phone, Kodak is virtually out of business. The Coca-Cola Company is under fire for allegedly causing obesity and is desperate to repair the image of its signature product. And McDonalds? In 2013, when it began soliciting positive customer comments on Twitter, it instead got overwhelmed with tweeted horror stories from the public, leading the campaign to be dubbed "McFail."

Technology and the internet have changed everything. That, in turn, means manufactured emotions delivered by an ad or a commercial will only get an organization so far these days. As the same Advertising Age article goes on to say, *"Our brands ask consumers for what a person expects from his or her friends—loyalty, trust, attention, love, time—without putting in the reciprocally requisite work. In other words, brands need to reconsider their motivations and behaviors because no one is buying the be-our-friend act any longer."*[28]

In other words, trying to manufacture an emotion without having anything real behind it just won't do the job for a business anymore.

That's why Mission-Driven Branding is a must for this day and age. When an organization genuinely takes on a mission and implements it inside and out, when it is consistent and authentic in pursuing that mission, that organization has a far greater chance of creating loyalty and trust – and of creating an *authentic* emotional response - than by

---

27. Walker, Abbie. "Brands Need to Know Their Purpose and What They Aspire to Be," Advertising Age, February 24, 2014.
28. Walker.

constantly reinventing its appeal with gimmicky short-term marketing campaigns.

There are two huge factors in play today that are an enormous threat to any company trying to win over customers and clients with superficial marketing tactics:

1. There's too much information out there.
Abraham Lincoln famously said, "You can fool all the people some of the time, and some of the people all the time, but you cannot fool all the people all the time." That's never been more true than right this minute.

For example, in Chapter 1 of this book, we discussed how Chick-fil-A got embroiled in a firestorm over its backing of anti-gay policies. At the time, a sweet-looking teenage girl rushed to the company's defense by writing earnest posts on her Facebook page detailing all of Chick-fil-A's wonderful qualities. But, because the internet is the internet, somebody quickly figured out that this girl's picture was licensed from a stock photo company - and the media presumed that Chick-Fil-A had most likely set up the fake account to manufacture support for its positions,[29] even with no real evidence to prove it.

In other words, whereas a brand might have been able to get away with these kinds of practices before, there is virtually no chance of it now. Even if Chick-fil-A hadn't put up the fake Facebook account, the internet "jury" still found the company guilty by association. And this was far from an isolated case – right now, there are now millions of amateur "branding police" actively investigating which companies are trying to pull a fast one and which ones are being authentic.

The Mission-Driven company has a natural advantage in this punitive climate. When it stays true to its mission, an organization can't help but pass the "smell test" on the internet and elsewhere. It earns respect rather than derision from its actions – and that respect boosts its brand above the competition.

---

29. Johnson, Dave. "Did Chick-fil-A's PR use fake Facebook account?" CBSNews.com, July 30, 2012. http://www.cbsnews.com/news/did-chick-fil-as-pr-use-fake-facebook-account/

2. There are too many choices out there.

With all the choices out there for a consumer, and all things being equal, how are is that person going to choose who to buy from? Or perhaps the bigger question is: *Why* would that person choose to buy from a certain company or individual over another?

Being Mission-Driven gives your company the answer to a customer's "Why." By defining how your brand uniquely serves the customer or society at large, you also define the positive *role* of your brand in that person's life.

Let's go back to a few of the brands we already talked about and see how their missions add value not only to the brands themselves, but also to a consumer's buying experience:

- If you want yummy ice cream *and* you want to make the world a better place, you buy from Ben & Jerry's.
- If you want a good chicken lunch or dinner *and* want to support a company that shares your values, you buy from Chick-fil-A.
- If you want a smartphone *and* want to buy from the company with the most innovative and stylish technology, you buy from Apple.

In each of the above cases, the company's mission gives the consumer a strong, concrete reason to buy from them – and to continue buying from them. There will always be plenty of premium ice cream brands, chicken restaurants and smartphone manufacturers to choose from – but Ben & Jerry's, Chick-fil-A and Apple all bring a whole lot more than their actual products to the consumer marketplace. No, their individual missions don't resonate with everyone – but they resonate strongly enough with a large enough base to keep their brands incredibly profitable and continually growing.

Again, being Mission-Driven is not really an option in today's marketplace - it's a necessity. As FastCoExist.com put it, "Today's brand must live and breathe through its core values in order to survive. Purpose is king, and there's no turning back."[30] And, in the words of Charles Schwab's executive vice president and CMO, Becky Saeger,

---

30. Blotter, Jennifer. "10 Ways Today's Purpose-Driven Brands Can Bring Their Core Values To Life," FastCoExist.com, October 14, 2013. http://www.fastcoexist.com/3019856/10-ways-todays-purpose-driven-brands-can-bring-their-core-values-to-life

"to be successful today, you must identify your company's purpose and execute like crazy."[31]

MISSION-DRIVEN BRANDING: HOW IT DELIVERS THE 5 BIG "D'S"

In the past few chapters, we've looked at how a Mission-Driven company realized rewards in its marketing and its business operation. We'd like to close this chapter by naming what we've identified as the "5 Big D's" - the 5 biggest benefits that a successful mission can bring to any brand.

• DESIRABILITY

As we saw in Chapter 2, the right mission attracts a fervent and loyal customer/client base all on its own. When that mission is organically attached to the brand in question, the brand not only attracts buyers, it also attracts quality employees who want to be a part of the brand's mission. Apple again is the best example of this principle in action, but there's no question the quality of Desirability applies to many, many other Mission-Driven brands as well, such as Disney, Patagonia, or Zappos.

• DISTANCE

Any brand faces the danger of losing its luster over time. Remember when Atari was the only gaming choice in American households? Or when you could find a Blockbuster video store in every strip mall in the neighborhood? In contrast, having a firm mission in place – and, just as importantly, continuing to make that mission relevant (imagine if Blockbuster had been the first to do what Netflix did) – almost guarantees consumer loyalty and an ongoing high profile in the marketplace, allowing a brand to truly go the *distance.*

• DEPENDABILITY

A mission helps a brand retain a consistent identity in the public's mind over the long haul. That consistency is important to developing trust and likeability with clients/customers and keeping them coming back for more. Walmart's "Always the Lowest Price" mission, for example, drives a constant stream of bargain-driven consumers

---

31. Adamson, Allen. "Define Your Brand's Purpose, Not Just Its Promise." Forbes, November 11, 2009.

through its doors, because those consumers know the retailer has a high degree of *dependability*.

• DIRECTION

A mission empowers a brand to focus on what it does best and provide a strong direction for the company as a whole. For instance, companies like Google and Apple understand they have a mandate to continue to deliver innovative technology that improves people's lives. That mandate, in turns, drives how they do business over the long haul and forces them to concentrate on the *direction* that defines them in terms of public perception.

• DIFFERENTIATION

Finally, Mission-Driven branding creates a powerful *differentiation* in the marketplace in contrast to the competition. Ben & Jerry's had that differentiation when they first began as a homegrown socially-aware business – and they quickly lost it when the brand became just another acquisition by a multinational corporation, Unilever. For those few years, they were just another ice cream brand – and it was easy for their formerly-fervent fans to simply pick another ice cream if it was cheaper or more convenient. A mission makes a company more than just another merchant or service provider – it transforms it into something much more meaningful and substantial, a business that truly stands out from the pack.

Of course, we've cherry-picked a lot of successful brands in this chapter to demonstrate the power of Mission-Driven branding. You the reader might rightly ask, "Well, yes, a mission works for big players like Apple and Google, but what real difference does it make to most companies?"

Well, we're glad you asked (even if we were the ones doing the asking for you) – because, it turns out, there is actually a concrete way to demonstrate the overall and overwhelming advantage of Mission-Driven branding.

In 2011, Havas Media Labs, one of the leading global communications and marketing groups, began compiling what they called the "Meaningful Brands Index." For the first time, a detailed analysis of companies that were Mission Driven in one way or another (through CSR (Corporate Social Responsibility) policies, sustainability, community giving, cause marketing, etc.) was done to determine just how this kind of brand activity affected their actual business.

The result? In the 2013 survey, the most recent one as of this writing, the so-called Meaningful Brands **outperformed the stock market by an incredible 120%.**[32]

Umair Haque, director of Havas Media Labs, had this to say as an explanation of the amazing success of Mission-Driven brands: "People aren't irrational in what they expect. They don't want perfect lives—but they do want better lives. What we consistently find is that institutions don't meet their expectations in real human terms. When they do find companies that are willing to benefit them, they're really happy doing business with them."[33]

Don't believe a business can *really* change the world for the better? Well, in our next chapter, we'll tell you exactly how some special Mission-Driven players upped their game - and scored a big win for all of us.

---

32. Dill, Kathryn. "Google, Samsung, Microsoft Head A Tech-Dominated List of The Most 'Meaningful' Brands," *Forbes*, June 14, 2013.
33. Dill

CHAPTER 5

HOW MISSIONS CREATE INCREDIBLE CHANGE

He was tired of being left out in the rain in the middle of the night in San Francisco.

As a young hotshot hi-tech entrepreneur, he would routinely be up late in a favorite restaurant, spit-balling new start-up ideas with other colleagues who were as ambitious and driven as him. Unfortunately, after those marathon sessions, he would find himself out in the street at 2 or 3 in the morning, unable to get a taxi to take him home.

That was a pain.

Suddenly, on a cold winter's night in Paris, the entrepreneur was doing yet another one of his late night brainstorming sessions, when he complained about the SF cab situation to his friend, another entrepreneur looking for something new to do. The situation sparked a thought for a start-up. A new kind of limo service. Maybe, when they got back to their home city, they could split the costs of a Mercedes, a driver and a space in a parking garage? Each man could access the car and driver when needed. If that worked out, they could expand the concept to other potential customers.

A couple years later, they were ready to bring the idea to life – only as more of a taxi substitute, rather than a limo service. That would bring more customers. They hired a general manager to work out the operational kinks - someone they had discovered from a tweet he had sent in response to one of theirs. Their first test? Well, it didn't happen in San Francisco. Instead, they sent three cars and drivers out to roam the SOHO/Chelsea/Union Square area in NYC. The cars could be summoned through a special smartphone app, which was given to a circle of select people. If everything went smoothly in New York, New York…well, as the song says, if they could make it there, they could make it anywhere.

New York proved the idea would work – so they prepared for a proper launch back in San Francisco a few months later. The service was an instant success and they were easily able to get additional financing to expand their new business. That success mushroomed to such an extent that more and more investors were banging on their door, ready to put in as much as it took to get a piece of what was looking like The Next Big Thing.

Big success, as it usually does, also brought some big new problems, however. A few months in, they were hit with a Cease and Desist order by the San Francisco Metro Transit Authority & the Public Utilities Commission of California for running a cab service without a license. Eventually, the entrepreneurs negotiated an agreement with the state agencies and agreed to take the word "cab" out of their company's name.

The service continued to lengthen its reach – it expanded back to New York City, and then continued on to Seattle, Chicago, Boston and Washington D.C. Even overseas to Paris, where the whole idea originated. And everywhere they took the service, it was an immediate hit. It became such a huge operation, that the company had enough clout to negotiate a deal with automakers to make vehicles more affordable for its drivers.

At the moment, Uber, which began life as UberCab, is valued at an estimated $40 billion dollars[34] and has almost completely changed the way people get around in metropolitan areas. In the San Francisco area alone, traditional taxi use has dropped 65%.[35] In New York, the price of a taxi medallion, which gives a driver a license to drive a cab,

---

34. MacMillan, Douglas. "Uber Snags $41 Billion Valuation," *The Wall Street Journal*, December 5, 2014.

35. Buckley, Sean. "The Uber effect: how San Francisco's cab use dropped 65-percent," Engadget.com, September 17, 2014 http://www.engadget.com/2014/09/17/sf-taxi-decline/

has dropped by 17%.[36] Other Uber-esque companies like Lyft have begun to spout all over the world. There is now even an Uber-type company for helicopters called Blade.

Uber's company mission had completely changed the transportation business model.

Here's a very powerful, liberating and, yes, scary, truth of life in the 21st Century: It's never been easier to change the world.

Think of the words that we all use on a daily basis today that didn't even exist ten or fifteen years ago, words like YouTube, Facebook and Twitter. The companies that brought these new words to life were able to quickly penetrate the public's consciousness at record-breaking speed simply because the internet exists – and they had found a new, fun and useful way to connect with its users.

And ironically, these social media tools, along with many others, now enable a company like Uber to also progress at a supersonic rate. It can happen so alarmingly fast that everyone involved can get a case of operational whiplash. The competition has to scramble to survive the new rules of business (a bad problem to have) – while the company that led the charge has to deal with overwhelming growth in a very short span of time (a *good* problem to have).

In this chapter, we're going to look at one of the ultimate benefits of a specific form of being Mission-Driven – and that's the capacity to create enormous change in the way an entire business sector operates. When a company chooses the right mission and implements it in the right way, it's not only able to create that change – it's also able to leverage it so that it's able to dominate its industry and experience incredible success.

How does an entrepreneur key into this incredibly powerful, profitable and pro-consumer positioning?

Here's the answer in two words – *Disruptive Innovation.*

---

36. Carr, David. "When the Forces of Disruption Hit Home," *The New York Times,* Monday, December 1, 2014.

UNDERSTANDING DISRUPTIVE INNOVATION

The buzzwords for what we're talking about in this chapter are "disruptive innovation" or "disruptive technology." Both terms were coined by Clayton M. Christensen, a professor at the Harvard Business School who first identified this kind of rapid and radical change in his best-selling 1997 book, *The Innovator's Dilemma*, which received the Global Business Book Award for the best business book of the year.

Christenson, identified by *Forbes* magazine as "one of the most influential business theorists of the last 50 years,"[37] first explained how big established companies could easily be brought down by smaller companies delivering the same service in a cheaper, more affordable and/or more convenient way. Uber, of course, is an excellent example of this process, but it's far from the only one in recent memory.

For example, remember when Encyclopedia Britannica used to sell you a set of encyclopedias for over $1000 – and then you'd be left with a set of giant, unwieldy books that together weighed over 100 pounds? Oh yeah, and *then* you'd have to wait a year for an updated version, at which point you'd have to spend another $1000 for another set of giant books?

That sounds like ancient history - even though it's only been since 2010 when the company finally gave up the ghost and stopped printing physical copies of their flagship product. And even though they still deliver their encyclopedic information online, Wikipedia.org (despite its occasional accuracy-challenged entries) delivers the exact same service absolutely free. As a matter of fact, Wikipedia is even more comprehensive and covers a wider array of topics – and even though it's a nonprofit, it still jumpstarted the disruptive innovation that brought a fatal blow to Encyclopedia Britannica's 230 year-old business model.

Now, disruptive innovation isn't new to this day and age. Henry Ford certainly disrupted the horse and buggy business when he first offered an affordable Model T in 1905. And Alexander Graham Bell certainly disrupted the Western Union telegraph business when he came up with the telephone (even though Western Union had the opportunity to buy all the telephone patents for $100,000 from Bell).

---

37. Whelan, David. "Clayton Christensen: The Survivor," *Forbes*, February 23, 2011.

The difference today? How quickly disruption can occur and how many different industries continue to be vulnerable to it. The internet, combined with the widespread usage of mobile devices, has enabled instant communication and incredible access to a wide variety of products and services – making it much easier for a new company to not only build a better mousetrap, but also quickly deliver it to your doorstep after you've punched a simple few keys on your smartphone.

Think about this stunning example of disruptive innovation: In 2003, Apple introduced the iPod along with the iTunes store. Both of these developments revolutionized the music industry and created two new giant markets for the company: the iPods and the *songs* to play on the iPods. In a span of only three years, the iPod and iTunes were bringing in $10 billion, which accounted for almost *half* of all of Apple's revenue. In 2003, Apple's market capitalization was roughly $1 billion. By the end of 2007? That figure was over $150 billion.[38]

THE KEYS TO EFFECTIVE DISRUPTION

When your mission is disruption, you should probably think about leaving your MBA at the door, if you have one. That's because, according to Christensen and his colleagues, creating disruptive innovation doesn't begin with traditional business models. No, this kind of company mission actually begins with what they call a Customer Value Proposition (CVP).[39] The CVP is all about analyzing what kind of "job" a customer needs to have done – and how to help that customer get it done in the best way possible. In the words of the Harvard Business Review, "Customer value propositions can be a guiding beacon as well as the cornerstone for superior business performance."[40]

By "job," the authors specifically are talking about how the customer would *prefer* to have a product or service sold or delivered - rather than the old-school traditional way it's always been done in the past. For an example, let's return to encyclopedias. Consumers, in order to get access to an encyclopedia's facts and figures in the past, had to spend a lot of money to get a very cumbersome product that quickly

---

38. Johnson, Mark W., Christensen, Clayton M. and Kagermann, Henning. "Reinventing Your Business Model," *Harvard Business Review*, December, 2008.

39. Johnson, Mark W., Christensen, Clayton M. and Kagermann, Henning cite

40. Anderson, James C, Narus, James A., and Van Rossum, Wouter, "Customer Value Propositions in Business Markets," *Harvard Business Review*, March 2006 issue

became outdated and obsolete. The "job" they really wanted to have done was to be able to get that same information quickly, affordably, and conveniently – a job Wikipedia accomplished like gangbusters.

The greatest opportunity for creating a powerful CVP comes when the job is important to the customer and the current alternatives to getting it done aren't very good. Another great example: The scenario we presented at the beginning of this chapter, in which a man standing out in the rain late at night in San Francisco can't get a taxi to take him home. Uber was expressly created to get that job done in a much better way – and their solution hit the CVP "sweet spot."

In the words of Christensen and his associates, *"Opportunities for creating a CVP are at their most potent, we have found, when alternative products and services have not been designed with the real job in mind and you can design an offering that gets that job—and only that job—done perfectly."*[41]

They also identified four obstacles that consumers generally face that a CVP should attempt to overcome:

- **Unaffordability**: The average consumer doesn't want to (or can't) pay the current price for a certain product or service.

- **Access**: Customers aren't able to easily obtain the product or service.

- **Skill:** Customers lack necessary professional training to get a job done, so they must hire someone who does.

- **Time:** The process of getting a product or service takes up too much of a customer's day.

Now, most CVPs can only address a couple of these barriers. For example, Uber solved the problems of access (the guy can't get a cab) and time (it takes too long for a cab to come if you call). But a product like QuickBooks, the small business software package, solved the problems of skill (small business owners could now do their own books), unaffordability (it cost mom and pop operations too much to hire accountants) and time (QuickBooks makes doing the books a lot more efficient and faster).

---

41. Johnson, Mark W., Christensen, Clayton M. and Kagermann, Henning

Technology enables many companies, particularly online retailers, to overcome all four. They create *affordability*, by allowing customers to crosscheck the prices of a wide range of products. They grant *access* by offering a wide range of products that you wouldn't find in a traditional brick-and-mortar store. They overcome a lack of *skill* in shopping, by offering recommendations and advice on what to purchase, and, of course, they also save *time* for customers by enabling them to pick products at their leisure when conventional stores might be closed, and get their purchases instantly shipped right to their homes or offices. This is the kind of disruptive innovation that allowed Zappos to dominate in online shoe sales, Warby Parker in online eyewear sales and Bonobos to become the largest clothing brand built on the web.

All of the above cases show that *focus* is an incredibly important element of a CVP. Whatever customer "job" your CVP tackles should be nailed down precisely and perfectly. There's a reason the online retailers we just listed all concentrate on just one particular type of apparel – it's easier to create and market a specific positive experience related to a single product category than it is to try and sell everything at once. Trying to do too many things will dilute your mission in the eyes of your potential clients/customers - and also compromise your ability to perform at a high level. Too often, when you try to do everything at once, you end up excelling at very little.

Now, you might respond to that, "What about Amazon? It sells everything and it's phenomenally successful." Well, we're glad you brought it up (even though we're the ones who actually did it for you) – because Amazon is actually the exception that proves *all* the rules we just discussed. And that's why we're going to close this chapter by taking a closer look at this incredible Mission-Driven company's disruptive ways.

AMAZON'S AMAZING WEAPONS OF MASS DISRUPTION

When it comes to carrying out disruptive innovative, Amazon brightly illuminates what works through the "Weapons of Mass Disruption" it has employed over the past twenty years. That means regularly changing up its mission – at least its public one – while secretly clinging to its actual one: Flat-out owning the commercial possibilities of cyberspace.

Don't believe that was the initial aim of Jeff Bezos, the founder of Amazon? Well, if you type "Relentless.com" in your web browser, you may change your mind – as the web address will take you directly to Amazon's website. That's because Jeff Bezos, the founder of Amazon, initially considered naming his world-famous internet business Relentless. Maybe he changed his mind because that name would have given away his ultimate game.

But let's not get ahead of ourselves. Instead, let's start with Bezos' first Weapon of Mass Disruption:

Weapon #1: Focus
Bezos began his professional life on Wall Street, where, in 1990, he became the youngest senior vice president at the investment firm D.E. Shaw. Four years later, however, he abruptly quit the world of high finance. He had always been fascinated by computers and he noted that usage of the internet was skyrocketing – in the past year, it had mushroomed by 230,000%.

To him, that meant the timing was excellent to try an online business.

Three years before anyone ever articulated the theory of disruptive innovation, Bezos instinctively knew he needed to have a narrow *focus* to his fledgling business. That focus became books. Since online shopping was still a very new and untested concept, he knew he had to make sure to offer the right product. Books turned out to be that product. In terms of costs, books were easy to ship and hard to break. There wouldn't be many returns or replacements necessary.

Weapon #2: Customer Value Proposition
As noted above, from a sheer operational standpoint, books were an excellent commodity to focus on for the launch of Amazon.com. They also provided, however, an equally excellent CVP.

In that regard, the main "job" it performed for its customers was providing incredible *access*. A physical bookstore could only stock so many different books – just a tiny fraction of all the books in print around the world. So, frequently, when a customer wandered into a bookstore looking for a specific title, the book would have to be ordered by the bookstore and the customer would have to return in a week or so to pick it up. With an online bookseller, however, *every single book in print* could be ordered online directly from Amazon and delivered right to the customer's home.

That powerful CVP allowed Amazon to become an instant success; the young company was already selling $20,000 worth of books in a week after only two months of being in business - and Bezos' first full year in business generated over half a million dollars in sales.

Weapon #3: A Long-Range Plan

Most consumers back in the early days of Amazon assumed Bezos' goal was simply to become THE online bookseller – which it quickly did. Amazon completely turned the traditional book-selling business model upside down. Over the past two decades, local bookstore after local bookstore has gone out of business, along with such big national book chains such as Borders, B. Dalton and Waldenbooks. Book-lovers have mourned that loss – but, at the same time, they hastened that loss, because they couldn't help but gravitate to the incredible choice of books that Amazon offered.

Owning web-based book sales was an incredible achievement all by itself – and, if the company only thought as far as Zappos, Warby Parker or Bonobos did, Amazon would have reached the end game of its disruptive innovation. But Bezos didn't care all that much about books – and certainly didn't want to be limited to only selling them.

Because being a bookseller was NOT his mission.

During the first year of its operation, Bezos ran an Amazon booth at a publishers' convention in Chicago. Roger Doeren, a bookstore owner from Kansas City, saw a sign at the booth that read, "Earth's Biggest Bookstore." According to a New Yorker article, Doeren wanted to find out more - and the conversation went like this:

Approaching Bezos, he asked, "Where is Earth's biggest bookstore?"

"Cyberspace," Bezos replied.

"We started a Web site last year. Who are your suppliers?"

"Ingram, and Baker & Taylor."

"Ours, too. What's your database?"

" 'Books in Print.' "

"Ours, too. So what makes you Earth's biggest?"

"We have the most affiliate links"—a form of online advertising.

Doeren considered this, then asked, "What's your business model?"

Bezos said that Amazon intended to sell books as a way of gathering data on affluent, educated shoppers. The books would be priced close to cost, in order to increase sales volume. After collecting data on millions of customers, Amazon could figure out how to sell everything else dirt cheap on the Internet.[42]

In other words, Bezos originally had a huge long-term disruptive goal: He wanted to sell everything under the sun and use the massive consumer data it was collecting from its book buyers to do it. And, of course, now Amazon sells everything from lawnmowers to diapers – and U.S. book sales only make up around 7% of its annual revenues. To quote that same New Yorker article, *"...books were Amazon's version of a gateway drug."*[43]

Weapon #4: Continually Building on Your Base

Earlier, we detailed how Apple upended the music business with its iPod and iTunes Store. Bezos couldn't help but take note as well – and wanted to make sure Apple didn't cut into his control of the cyber book market. In 2004, he set up a lab in Silicon Valley to build the first home-grown piece of technology for the company. In 2007, the result was the unveiling of the Amazon Kindle e-reader, which could be used to download and read digital versions of books. It did, in fact, further Amazon's disruptive innovation by making physical copies of books unnecessary. By 2010, Amazon controlled 90% of the new industry it had created, the digital book.

The development of the Kindle also provided Amazon with an entirely new revenue opportunity. Just as the selling of books opened up all areas of ecommerce to Bezos, the Kindle resulted in Amazon being taken seriously as a provider of technology. A few years later, Amazon released the Kindle Fire, a competitor to the Apple iPad. The company now has its own smartphone (which has yet to gain much traction) and

---

42. Packer, George. "Cheap Words," *The New Yorker*, February 17, 2014
43. Packer

is now producing its own content, including original programming and films designed to compete with Netflix offerings.

What is clear from this chapter is the right business mission can be hugely beneficial for both consumers and entrepreneurs. Consumers get what they want more easily and the businesses who make this happen are rewarded with a dominant position in the marketplace – if, like Steve Jobs or Jeff Bezos, they're smart enough to capitalize on that position.

In the past few chapters, we've detailed the plentiful and powerful benefits of being Mission-Driven. Now, in the next section of this book, it's your turn to find out how you can make your business or nonprofit a Mission-Driven success as well. We'll also be sharing our 3 Stage process to implement Mission-Driven principles into your life and your organization, as well as providing you with an interactive Action Guide designed to help you through the initial steps.

So get ready – your mission is only just beginning!

BOOK 2

YOUR MISSION*:
AN ACTION GUIDE
(Should you decide to accept it…)

"The two most important days in your life are the day you are born and the day you find out why."

~ Mark Twain

CHAPTER 6

THE 3-STAGE MISSION-DRIVEN ACTION PROCESS

The brand was at a standstill.

Dove Soap, a product created in 1953 by Lever Brothers, had been a steady seller since its inception. Its innovative "beauty bar," a soap that was composed of one-quarter cleansing cream, was sold on the basis of straightforward marketing messages touting its uniqueness. Taglines such as "Dove Won't Dry Your Skin Like Soap Can" and "Dove is Good for Your Skin" had a built-in appeal to its female target audience, and, by the 1990's, it was a 200 million dollar brand.

By the early 2000's, however, Dove had seemingly flown as high as it could with its traditional marketing approach. Up until then, the beauty brand, like its competition, had always used attractive models to demonstrate its product – but more and more, those attractive models seemed like an alien species to the majority of women. Result? Dove seemed like a dated commodity that was quickly losing its luster.

So – how could the 1950's beauty bar be made relevant in the 21st Century?

Unilever, which had absorbed Lever Brothers a decade earlier, decided rather than simply introduce a new glitzy marketing campaign, it was time to dig deeper – and actually reexamine what exactly beauty meant to women in this day and age. That was the kind of undertaking that would require a great deal of time, effort and money; the multinational corporation was willing to commit to a heavy investment in all three.

Unilever commissioned a global study on the uneasy relationship between women and their appearance. And this study was the real deal, based on quantitative data collected from a global study of 3,200 women, aged 18 to 64. StrategyOne, an applied research firm based in New York, managed the study in collaboration with Harvard University and the London School of Economics. Interviews were conducted across ten countries: the U.S., Canada, Great Britain, Italy, France, Portugal, Netherlands, Brazil, Argentina and Japan. And never once was the Dove brand mentioned or alluded to in any of these interviews.

In other words, this was not brand research – this was *human* research.

And the results were fairly shocking. Only 2% of the women respondents felt comfortable describing themselves as "beautiful." 40% of women "strongly disagreed" that they were beautiful.[44] The conclusion of the study came down to this: "The definition of beauty had become limiting and unattainable."[45] That meant Dove had to figure out how to sell a beauty product to women who didn't think of themselves as beautiful.

The company's solution? Expand the definition of beauty.

That effort began with a revolutionary photo exhibit, "Beyond Compare: Women Photographers on Real Beauty," a show organized by Dove and Ogilvy & Mather. The showing featured work from world-famous female photographers showcasing so-called "ordinary women," photographed like models. In 2005, this concept expanded into a print campaign also centered on portraying real women with real bodies, but treating them as though they were professional models in print ads and photos.

This attention-getting approach generated such huge media conversations both in social media and on television talk shows that

44. "The Real Truth about Beauty: A Global Report" - Findings of the Global Study on Women, Beauty and Well-Being, September 2004, available at http://www.clubofamster-dam.com/contentarticles/52%20Beauty/dove_white_paper_final.pdf
45. http://www.dove.us/Social-Mission/campaign-for-real-beauty.aspx

Dove's ad agency estimated it got 30 times the marketing value from the ad space it purchased. That success prompted a continuation and expansion of the campaign. In 2006, Dove produced several compelling videos chronicling the world's unrealistic expectations of female beauty – all of which went viral. One of them, "Evolution," alone garnered over 18 million views on YouTube.[46] Dove further cemented its commitment to this social issue by aligning itself with the Girl Scouts, the Boys and Girls Clubs of America and Girls Inc. to promote self-esteem in girls about their looks.

Dove's Real Beauty campaign continues to this day, attracting enormous media attention and creating heated controversy. Their Facebook page alone has 19 million "likes." According to Sharon MacLeod, vice president of Unilever North America Personal Care, "The conversation is as relevant and fresh today as it was 10 years ago, I believe we'll be doing this campaign 10 years from now."[47]

Why is she so sure about that? Perhaps because the former $200-million-dollar-a-year brand is now worth about $4 *billion* – purely as a result of the company transforming itself from an everyday soap seller into a Mission-Driven Brand.

If you're still in doubt about what the power of a mission can do for a nuts-and-bolts business, the preceding Dove story can't help but force you to rethink that opinion. If a fifty year-old fading soap company can completely reinvigorate its image and become one of the most talked-about brands of our times – simply by taking on a mission that's more about sociology than marketing - it's hard to see why any other kind of business would be unable to do the same, no matter how old or seemingly set in its ways it happens to be.

Does that include *your* business?

Think about it. What if you were to become a Mission-Driven business? How might a mission transform both your brand and your business results? How might it attract a whole new base of customers and clients – as well as boost your profile and your prestige?

46. https://www.youtube.com/watch?v=iYhCn0jf46U
47. Bahadur, Nina. "Dove 'Real Beauty' Campaign Turns 10: How A Brand Tried To Change The Conversation About Female Beauty," The Huffington Post, January 21, 2014 http://www.huffingtonpost.com/2014/01/21/dove-real-beauty-campaign-turns-10_n_4575940.html

We want to help you explore your Mission-Driven possibilities. To that end, we're about to provide you with a 3-Stage Action Process that will deliver to you a personalized blueprint for your own Mission-Driven business. Even if you *already* run a business, then we'll help you adapt it to a Mission-Driven one (in the same way that Dove Soap did in the story that opened this chapter).

Before we get into that section of this book, however, we'd like to explain that this process comes out of our work with more than 2000 clients that we've worked with in our agency. Our interest is always in helping them develop the potential of their businesses to the fullest. That's of course not an entirely altruistic impulse on our part – because, frankly, if our clients don't succeed, we don't succeed.

One of the easiest ways for us to set the foundation for our process is to relate it to a concept you've likely already heard of. That concept is entitled "The Golden Circle," articulated in a world-famous TED talk given by ex-advertising executive Simon Sinek.[48] The basis of the Golden Circle is Sinek's analysis of the reason many of the world's most effective individuals and companies find such high levels of success. His research demonstrated that success is a result of "Inside-Out" thinking – a progression from "Why" to "How" to, finally, "What."

Here's Sinek's graphic representation of this progression:

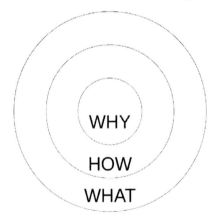

The successful people and companies Sinek profiles always start with the "Why"; in other words, before they started out towards a major accomplishment, they keyed into their inner passions and what mattered to them most. Their next step was to figure out "How" they were going to line up their life direction in a vehicle to accomplish those passions – and then, finally, they would take a look at "What" they were going to do to bring all that to fruition.

How is that different from most people's approaches? According to Sinek, too many individuals instead start with their "What," leading them into lives with which they don't feel a real connection. These are the kinds of people that take a job simply to have a job and don't make enough of an effort to explore what they *really* want to do. Granted, we all have to do things to support ourselves, but when that short-term need dominates our long-term lives, we often dull the real individual power that comes from our intuition and true inner motivations.

What appeals to us about Sinek's model is it provides the perfect path for taking a personal mission from the theoretical to the practical. An idea isn't really worth a lot until you find a way to actually put it to work in the real world – and we've developed a process designed to do just that, and as you'll see, it aligns very well with Sinek's "Why," "How" and "What" progression.

Now, let's go more into detail about the 3 stages of our Action Process.

STAGE ONE: YOUR "WHY"
— DISCOVERING YOUR LIFE MISSION

This is where it all begins.

Your Life Mission lays the foundation of your Mission-Driven organization. It represents one or more aspects of what you care about the most – your deepest passion, your greatest talent and/or your biggest social concern. Your Life Mission is your greatest motivator to both dream and achieve.

Here are three historic figures who have readily identifiable Life Missions that you're almost certainly already aware of:

- **Mother Theresa:** To continually help the poor and needy.

- **Mahatma Gandhi:** To fight for justice, freedom and dignity for all.

- **Steve Jobs:** A relentless drive to create and innovate with technology.

In the case of all three of the above individuals, most people immediately think of their Life Mission when they hear their names. It defined them more than anything else about them.

The right Life Mission will do the same for you. It will make you identifiable and memorable – as well as shape others' opinions of you. It will also draw supporters to your side and create a directed energy that helps you clear a strong and specific path. But your Life Mission will only succeed at all that if comes from something strong and authentic within you.

The bottom line is your Life Mission is your "Why." It ties directly into your life motivations as well as your greatest enthusiasms in your day-to-day life.

It's what gives you *purpose*.

STAGE TWO: YOUR "HOW" — FINDING THE VEHICLE TO ACTIVATE YOUR LIFE MISSION

If your Life Mission represents the idealistic "Why" that motivates you, then your company or non-profit represents the practical *Vehicle* that becomes "How" – the way you work towards your Life Mission in the real world.

For example, you might be someone who in general loves gourmet food – that's your Life Mission. But what do you do with that love – how do you fulfill your Life Mission? Do you open a restaurant? Become a chef? Or a food critic? The choice of Vehicle (the type of company of non-profit) for your Life Mission will most likely be made based on your other talents, interests, resources and opportunities.

More on that later. For now, let's take the three individuals whose Life Missions we just described – and talk about the Vehicles they used to realize them.

- Mother Theresa decided her Life Mission to help the needy needed as its Vehicle an infrastructure to enable her to help the impoverished on a global level. With that in mind, she founded the Missionaries of Charity, a Roman Catholic religious congregation, which currently consists of over 4,500 sisters and operates health clinics and programs for the disadvantaged in over 130 countries.

- Gandhi's Life Mission of justice and freedom drove him to lead India to gain independence from British rule. He used as his Vehicle political power by working with the Indian Congress to build his national influence, and then, in turn, inspiring his countrymen to participate in mass protests demanding self-governance for India.

- Steve Jobs' Life Mission to innovate found its Vehicle through the founding and running Apple, and leading that corporation to release a steady stream of groundbreaking and ridiculously successful products.

In each case, an authentic Life Mission manifested itself in a Vehicle that allowed the accomplishment of the mission. Your Vehicle therefore, is your "How" – it's how your Life Mission gets out of your brain and into the world.

STAGE THREE: YOUR "WHAT"
— DETERMINING YOUR ANNUAL CAMPAIGN

Rome wasn't built in a day. And you certainly can't accomplish a true Life Mission in 24 hours or less either. That's why you need to figure out "What" to do with your Vehicle to move towards your Life Mission in a thought-out step-by-step process.

Many people get caught up in the fact that they aren't able to visualize what their life or business will look like in 5, 10, 15, or even 20 years. While we absolutely think it's important to have long-term goals, we also don't want your inability to see the future (believe us, we can't either!) to keep you from getting started. Creating a series of short-term plans designed to take you closer to your ultimate ambitions also enables you to change up things more easily when the unexpected throws you for a loop. Because, as former boxer Mike Tyson once said, "Everybody has a plan until they get punched in the mouth." In life and business, we often get some blows we didn't expect, which is why we believe employing *Annual Campaigns* is the best ongoing strategy.

In our mind, every single calendar year a new Annual Campaign should be put into place that will enable a company or nonprofit to reach some significant benchmark in the effort to reach its Life Mission. This is where the rubber meets the road; practicality is the order of the day and a nuts-and-bolts approach must be found that everyone you work with can understand and get on board with. The calendar year is an arbitrary choice of time and sometimes changes occur even faster, but it is a forced time to keep you on track.

If you've read or seen any of the numerous Steve Jobs' biographies, you know that this man drove Apple execs and employees to deliver what he knew he wanted. From the iMac to iTunes to the iPod and the iPhone, he constantly provided an updated Annual Campaign to take the company to the next level. Now, he didn't specifically call it that, but there *is* a reason why Apple holds its Worldwide Developer Conference once a year; it's the same reason many other companies host annual gatherings and conferences. It's a whole lot easier to think in one year increments than it is to plot out a complete path towards a lifetime ambition.

From the Life Mission to the Vehicle to a series of Annual Missions, the Mission-Driven process progresses from your innermost passions to incremental real-world stages that bring your Life Mission to life in a substantial and concrete way. Simply put, it's "What" you need to do within your Vehicle to reach your goals.

This, then, is our version of the Golden Circle we discussed earlier:

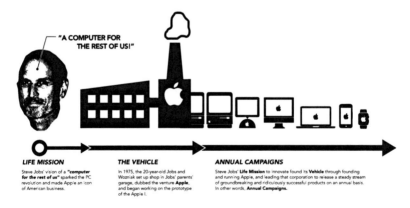

"A COMPUTER FOR THE REST OF US!"

LIFE MISSION
Steve Jobs' vision of a **"computer for the rest of us"** sparked the PC revolution and made Apple an icon of American business.

THE VEHICLE
In 1975, the 20-year-old Jobs and Wozniak set up shop in Jobs' parents' garage, dubbed the venture **Apple**, and began working on the prototype of the Apple I.

ANNUAL CAMPAIGNS
Steve Jobs' **Life Mission** to innovate found its **Vehicle** through founding and running Apple, and leading that corporation to release a steady stream of groundbreaking and ridiculously successful products on an annual basis. In other words, **Annual Campaigns.**

As the graphic illustrates, the Life Mission starts deep within you, from vital aspects of your identity (your "Why"). The Vehicle then helps you connect your Life Mission to the outside world through an infrastructure designed with that in mind (your "How"). Finally, your Annual Campaigns are engineered to move you closer and closer to your Life Mission through practical steps (your "What"). In this progression, you start from a place of pure ideals – and finally discover how you can put them to work in a less-than-ideal society.

Now that we've outlined this process, we want to help you work through it yourself – right here and right now. We're assuming you don't want to write directly in this book (you'll really find that difficult if you downloaded a digital copy of it!) – so you might want to have a notebook handy to follow through on the questions and exercises we're about to present.

So turn the page – and we'll start to explore the real you in the first stage of our Action Guide.

ACTION GUIDE STAGE 1: UNCOVERING YOUR LIFE MISSION

"Writing or reviewing a mission statement changes you because it forces you to think through your priorities deeply, carefully, and to align your behavior with your beliefs"

~ Stephen Covey, *7 Habits of Highly Effective People*

When the legendary Frank Sinatra was in his late teens, he happened to go to the movies – and caught then-superstar Bing Crosby crooning in a 1930's movie musical. Boom - Sinatra instantly knew his Life Mission was to become a singing sensation like Crosby. He then put all his energies into that goal to the point where he surpassed not only Crosby's success, but also his longevity.

It can be that simple. Many lucky individuals are either born knowing their life mission – or, like Sinatra, discover it early enough in life that they're never conflicted about the path they want to pursue.

For most of us, however, it takes some time and exploration. There are even those that don't really find their Life Mission until late in life. The celebrated American folk artist "Grandma Moses" didn't begin painting until the age of 78 – and only then became internationally famous for her talent. To this day, her work is still greatly appreciated – in 2006, her painting, *The Sugaring Off,* was sold for $1.2 million.

What's important, if you are unsure of what your Life Mission happens to be, is to not give up the quest. It's crucial not only for the purposes of this exercise – but for your own happiness and health. In 2014, the National Institute on Aging released the results of a study in which 60,000 people were surveyed. The results indicated that those having a definite purpose in life were more insulated from the harmful effects of stress and also tended to outlive their peers.[49] The study also showed that it didn't matter *when* in life someone found their Life Mission, they could still enjoy its beneficial effects once they did.

Action Step A: The Obituary Test

A great way to begin to unlock your Life Mission is to take what we call the Obituary Test. We talked about it more in detail in our previous book, *StorySelling*™ in regards to developing a business narrative, but the test works just as well (if not better) in this instance.

The Obituary Test was created by author Klaus Fog[50] and it's a great mental exercise that motivates you to examine your mindset from an entirely different perspective. It's also very simple – you just have to consider, and write down, what you would like to see included in your obituary after you've passed on. Yes, we know it's not fun to contemplate the end of your days, but using this thought process can help you zero in on what's really and truly important to you.

So go ahead – write your obituary as if you had "shuffled off this mortal coil" and accomplished the kinds of things that are near and dear to your heart. And as you do so, keep in mind these two pivotal questions:

- What specifically about you would have made you different from other people? Were you humorous and entertaining? Insightful and well-informed? Aggressive and able to make things happen?

- What are the biggest achievements you would want people to remember you for? Your altruistic works? Your game-changing business ventures? Your ability to mediate and negotiate between powerful parties? The family you helped create? Or, more typically, a combination of these things?

---

49. Neighmond, Patti, "People Who Feel They Have A Purpose In Life Live Longer," NPR Health News, July 28, 2014, http://www.npr.org/blogs/health/2014/07/28/334447274/people-who-feel-they-have-a-purpose-in-life-live-longer

50. Klaus Fog, *Storytelling: Branding in Practice*, (Springer Heidelberg Dordrecht 2010), p. 72

Approach the Obituary Test seriously – and be *honest* when you do it. You don't have to be embarrassed about what you write, nobody else has to see this except you (although it would be great if you shared it with people you trust and who know you well, to get their honest reactions). So let loose with your inner feelings and see what you end up with on the page. You should make a definite effort towards being extremely candid with yourself.

You should also put some effort into creating the correct *headline* for your obituary – the first thing people would write about you, based on who they felt you were. Think about when we listed the names of Steve Jobs, Mother Theresa and Mahatma Gandhi – and how certain images and thoughts immediately leaped into your mind. How would people sum you up – or, perhaps more importantly, how would you *want* them to sum you up if you followed through on your true desires?

So go ahead and write that obituary – and then we'll go back to dealing with you as a live and breathing human being (which should be a relief!). Hopefully this Action Step will open your mind to this line of thought and also help you uncover some of the traits of what business coach Dan Sullivan calls your "Unique Ability®[51]" – that collection of skills, passions, and talents that are uniquely your own. From that Unique Ability® will spring your Life Mission, so let's move on to our next Action Step and zero in on that area.

Action Step B: Creating Your Word Cloud
In this Action Step, we'll further hone in on the qualities that will inform your Life Mission. To do that, we'd like to ask you to fill out the following form, which contains 12 questions. We suggest you answer them as quickly as possible, each within 30 seconds if you can, to avoid second-guessing your initial impulse, which will probably be the truest one. Also – be brief. Don't be afraid of using the same words in different answers if they apply – that's actually part of the idea here.

---

51. Unique Ability® is a registered trademark of Strategic Coach®

IDENTIFYING YOUR PASSIONS

1. Name three things that make you the happiest. (This can be specific relationships, achievements, specific events, etc.)

1. _____

2. _____

3. _____

2. What are three of your favorite things to do, given the choice of anything in the world?

1. _____

2. _____

3. _____

3. Name three things you do that make you feel the best about yourself.

1. _____

2. _____

3. _____

4. Which three of your personal qualities are you most proud of?

1. _____

2. _____

3. _____

5. Think of your personal heroes – name three things about them that inspire you.

1. _____

2. _____

3. _____

6. What do you believe your three greatest natural gifts are?
(These can include talents, personality qualities, even your looks.)

1. _____

2. _____

3. _____

7. Identify three things that people look to you for? (In other words, what would they trust you to provide them? Advice? A sympathetic ear? Expertise in some area? A political opinion? Musical talent or some other creative skill?)

1. _____

2. _____

3. _____

8. What do you at this point in your life most regret not doing?

_____

9. What three causes do you most support?

1. _____

2. _____

3. _____

10. Name three ways you can best help those causes.

1. _____

2. _____

3. _____

11. What are your three strongest values?

1. _____

2. _____

3. _____

12. What, if anything, do you consider yourself an expert on? (If more than one thing, name them all)

_____

_____

After you've answered all of the 12 questions, we'd like you to now move on to the next part of this exercise – and create a "word cloud" of sorts. If you don't know what a word cloud is, it's a graphic representation of the most important ideas in text.

For example, here's a word cloud representation of the text from the 1776 Declaration of Independence:

abolishing absolute acts alter assent becomes colonies connected consent declare dissolved establishing ... foreign form free **government** ... hold independent justice large laws legislative legislature mankind nature offices others pass peace people powers ... protection refused repeated rights ... seas separation states suffer suspended ... usurpations war world

You'll see the most prominent words are the ones that most strongly represent the content of that historic document – with no words greater than "people," "laws" and "government."

What we'd like you to do is take the answers from the 12 questions and put them in this kind of word cloud format. Simply cut and paste all the text from your answers into a word cloud generator (there are tons of free ones on the internet – we used one at www.tagcrowd.com for our purposes) and you should end up with a visual representation of the things that are most important to you in life.

(You may find that your answers are simple one or two-word answers and don't really lend themselves to the word cloud process. In that case, simply rank your answers on a scale of 1 to 5, 5 being the answers about which you feel the strongest, 1 being the answers about which you're the least passionate. Simply list them in order from the 5's all the way to the 1's).

Action Step C: Writing Your Life Mission Statement

Now, you should be ready to take a stab at creating your very own preliminary Life Mission Statement - a very simple one-to-two line manifesto that lays out which of your qualities, talents and passions you want to use towards what abstract, broad-based goal.

To do that, first examine the most powerful words from your personal "word cloud." From them, create an *action line* that taps into your strengths and passions.

For example, let's say Brad Pitt had answered our 12 questions when he was just starting out in his career. And let's pretend some of the words that stood out from his answers were *"acting," "good-looking," and "charming."*

From that, he might determine, *"I'm going to use my looks, personality and talent..."* That action line would be the first part of his Life Mission Statement.

To devise the second part, you want to think about your *desired outcome* that your action line will bring about. Let's return to Brad Pitt and see how he might have handled it. Let's say some other strong words that resulted from his answers to the 12 questions were *"Hollywood," "acting," and "movies."*

From those words, he could continue his Life Mission statement with his desired outcome:

"I'm going to use my looks, personality and talent to become a movie star..."

Now, for the third and final part of his Life Mission statement, Brad would want to consider what he would want to do with his movie star status. In other words, what sort of *resulting impact* would he like to make with that position? He would then tap into a few other words that came out of his word cloud – words like, perhaps, *"social good,"* *"fame and fortune,"* *"artistic satisfaction."*

With those words in mind, he could have added on a resulting impact to complete his Life Mission Statement:

"I'm going to use my looks, personality and talent to become a movie star...which will give me the power to do movies I want to do and promote causes I feel strongly about."

And voila - you have a very viable Life Mission Statement (if you're Brad Pitt anyway).

Yes, we reverse-engineered that, but this will give you a sense of how putting together a Life Mission Statement works. When you're putting yours together, remember that you don't have to be locked into the first thing you write down. A Life Mission Statement is something you should give a lot of thought to, discuss with those you love and trust, until it's fine-tuned to something you truly feel represents your LM.

Of course, we're not all Brad Pitt, a fact that at least the two of us are painfully aware of. But there is always a way to put together a viable Life Mission Statement out of your personal "word cloud," no matter how unlikely a connection your words seem to have.

Now...it's your turn to try.

CONSTRUCTING YOUR LIFE MISSION STATEMENT

Action Line: *(What are your strongest abilities, talents and gifts)*

_____

_____

Desired Outcome: *(Where do you want these abilities, talents and gifts to take you?)*

_____

_____

_____

Resulting Impact: *(What do you want your outcome to achieve in the world or for your business?)*

_____

_____

_____

Completed Life Mission Statement:

_____

_____

_____

_____

_____

_____

Again – sometimes you can make the most unlikely combinations of abilities and ambitions work for you, so don't give up if at first you can't quite create a Life Mission Statement that works.

For instance, let's say you were a skilled winemaker. You love to ferment grapes and people love the way you do it. Now, let's complicate things a little. Let's say your second biggest passion is dogs – specifically the saving of poor stray pooches who are put in shelters.

Now, what in the world do we do with all that? Can you really create a Life Mission Statement that reads, *"I want to use my talent and skills in order to create a line of wines - that will benefit dogs"?*

Well, it turns out you can. And, a little later, we'll tell you more about how that happened.

CHAPTER 7

FUELING YOUR VEHICLE

While in college, he wrote a term paper on the need for a special overnight delivery service, since he believed society was entering a computerized information age. He detailed how the idea could be made to work. His professor wasn't convinced – and gave him a "C" on the paper.

It was another setback for a boy who had already experienced many. He was born with a congenital birth defect, as well as a hip disorder that forced him to wear braces and walk with crutches for most of his boyhood. He was to face a conflict of a much different sort after college, when, as a Marine, he was sent to serve in the Vietnam War and became a platoon leader. There he learned some important leadership lessons as he was put in charge of a group of soldiers with very different backgrounds and personalities. Vietnam also sparked a passion to build, after he saw so much useless destruction.

His first job, after leaving the service, was working for his stepfather, a retired Air Force general who had a company that overhauled older aircraft and modified their engines. That didn't last long, so he thought again about his overnight delivery idea. He went back to the plans he laid out in his term paper, a "hub and spokes" proposal in which packages from all over America would come to a central location, and then be flown out at night when airports were fairly empty.

When he inherited $4 million when his father passed away, he put it all into starting his "unfeasible" business. In 1971, his company was finally airborne - and became a huge overnight success. That's when Fred Smith decided to do something really radical with his already-revolutionary business, Federal Express.

Smith knew that, in order to guarantee the best delivery service, he had to create a unique relationship with the employees the company relied on to make it excel. In his mind, if his people were made a part of the decision-making processes and treated as well as possible, they would perform at a higher level and, as a result, increase business revenues. He called it the PSP philosophy (People-Service-Profit) and, in 1973, its implementation caused FedEx to become one of the first companies in the world to formally view employees as a means for achieving long-term growth.

The next step was to manifest that philosophy to both the employees as well as the outside world. To accomplish that, FedEx went ahead and created "The Purple Promise," which played off the color of the company's logo and consisted of only seven words: "I will make every FedEx experience outstanding."

Smith's term paper may have gotten a "C," but no rational business analyst would give the company he built that low a grade. The company has become the number one overnight delivery service in the world, handling more than 3 million packages in over 200 nations every single business day. Not only that, but in 2013, Fortune magazine named FedEx one of the top companies to work for.[52]

FedEx truly succeeding in making PSP its company-wide mission. In the words of its website, "The Purple Promise is more than what we say — it's what we do. It unites us. Every one of us at FedEx is committed to making every experience outstanding."[53]

As we noted, once you have your Life Mission in place, you need to find the Vehicle – the structured organization that will enable you to pursue your Life Mission. Well, just as important is discovering what *fuel* will power your vehicle onward towards your ultimate aims.

---

52. http://archive.fortune.com/magazines/fortune/best-companies/2013/list/
53. http://www.fedex.com/purplepromise/docs//en/fedex_pp_booklet.pdf

We suspect many of you reading this book already have a Vehicle in place and are looking for what exactly will move it forward in the direction you want it to go. Well, that's where the fuel comes in. For example, Fred Smith actually discovered his "fuel" of outstanding customer service *after* he created his Vehicle – which was the FedEx Corporation. In the case of Dove (which we related in Chapter 6), that company found tackling the whole concept of what constitutes female beauty was an excellent fuel to power its existing Vehicle.

In a little bit, we'll provide you with the second stage of your Action Guide so you can begin to identify what kind of fuel will do the trick for you. But first, we want to spend a little time discussing the different kinds of fuels we've identified that will give you the best mileage in your Vehicle of choice.

THE THREE TYPES OF FUELS

Our research has shown us that the most effective fuels fall into three main categories, which we're about to reveal. As you read through these, consider which type might work best for your specific Life Mission and Vehicle.

- **Fuel Type #1: Social Benefit**
  When a company uses Social Benefit as fuel for its Vehicle, it's specifically tooled to improve life at a local, national or even international level; those altruistic aims, in turn, draw consumers to its side, which powers the company to success. Both Ben & Jerry's as well as Newman's Own, two companies we've already talked about at length, are fueled by charitable goals that, as we've discussed, have very little to do with the actual food products these brands sell. However, the Social Benefit can directly tie in with the product, as in the cases of the previously-discussed Dove or Patagonia, and still achieve extremely powerful results.

- **Fuel Type #2: Buyer Benefit**
  Your Vehicle can also be fueled by an extremely high octane Buyer Benefit, in which you grant your customers and clients a clear and distinct advantage over buying from a competitor. As we've already noted, Fed Ex and Zappos both use this fuel; other similar ways of using it include Walmart's low price guarantee, Ebay's auction process and Amazon's extensive selection of products. In each of

these cases, the business is committed to a huge Buyer Benefit similar companies can't or won't offer, which gives its brands a huge defining positive that creates ongoing success.

- **Fuel Type #3: Disruptive Innovation**
  You might call Disruptive Innovation an alternative fuel, as it's designed to reboot an individual industry in a way that captures the public's imagination; huge, relatively new and explosively fast-growing companies such as Uber, PayPal and Amazon come to mind here. Disruptive Innovation does, however, shares some common properties with Buyer Benefit – because it does involve finding a way to serve the customer at a higher level. The difference, however, is the benefit a disruptive company delivers is far more wide-ranging; it's actually a radically new way of operating a traditional business, such as the way Uber turned the traditional taxi business on its head.

Now that you understand a little more about the types of fuels and how they work, let's move on to our next Action Guide that will help you determine which fuel will best power your organizational Vehicle – and how to activate a GPS that will get it to its destination.

ACTION GUIDE STAGE 2: CHOOSING YOUR FUEL AND DIRECTING YOUR VEHICLE

"If the risk is fully aligned with your purpose and mission, then it's worth considering."

~ Peter Diamandis

There are all kinds of vehicles in the world – everything from cars to motorcycles to trucks to - running on all kinds of fuels (everything from gas to electricity to hydrogen). It's no different when we talk about Mission-Driven Vehicles. There are many different kinds which use many varied fuel formulations.

For example, remember when we talked about the guy who had a Life Mission that revolved around making wine to benefit dogs? That may have seemed absurd to those of you who haven't heard of Chateau La Paws.

Chateau La Paws is a wine label created by Marty Spate, who has had a lifelong love of Man's Best Friend – as well as 16 years of winemaking experience. And he did, in fact, manage to find a way to combine those two Life Missions into a powerful Vehicle, with a line of wine varietals uncorked in early 2015. The labels on all their wine bottles feature portraits of various rescue dogs, photographed by acclaimed photographer Carli Davidson with the help of animal behaviorist Amanda Giese, who, according to the company, "worked tirelessly to capture each dog's personality."

The fuel? Well, that was of the Social Benefit variety. Chateau La Paws uncorked its label with an official national partnership in place with the North Shore Animal League America (NSALA), the world's largest no-kill animal rescue and adoption organization. The company committed to giving the NSALA a $100,000 donation in 2015 and plans to make additional commitments in the future. And of course, the cute shelter dogs featured on the wine label attracts attention to these poor pooches' plight in a big way.

And what does it do for the bottom line of Chateau La Paws?

Well, as you can imagine, every dog lover who spots one of the winemaker's pups on its label will immediately be interested in trying out the wine – especially when they read the little notice attached to every bottle that outlines the NSALA partnership. And if the quality doesn't bite (pun intended…sorry, we couldn't help ourselves), that dog lover will continue to buy more bottles as needed.

Yes, dogs and wine can be considered strange bedfellows – but they can be combined to create an unusual but very powerful custom-fit Vehicle that will travel a long way.

So let's see if we can determine the right fuel and the right destination for your specific Vehicle, based on the Life Mission to which you've dedicated yourself.

ACTION STEP A: CHOOSING YOUR FUEL TYPE

The best way to begin customizing your Vehicle is to determine what fuel type will help it run the most smoothly. If you already think you know which one is best for your Vehicle, we still suggest you go through the following three questionnaires we're about to share with you to make sure.

• Fuel Type #1: Social Benefit
To determine if a Social Benefit fuel is the right option for your Vehicle, ask yourself these questions:

Does my Life Mission contain a belief system, movement or cause I'm passionate about?

This could be as specific as being a dog lover (the creator of Chateau La Paws) to being a broader belief system (such as the founding family of Chick-fil-A, who made their Christian faith a major component of how they do business, as discussed in a previous chapter).

Will this particular fuel formula appeal to others?

A Social Benefit-based fuel only works if it attracts others to your side. If you feel strongly that Martians are about to visit earth and crown you king or queen of the planet, that most likely has a very limited appeal to others (of course, if this does in fact happen, let us be the first to apologize to you in advance, Your Majesty). There should be enough other people interested in your specific Social Benefit to make it viable.

Is there a compelling way to make this cause an aspect of a business?

As this is a business-oriented book, we're skipping past the Gandhi's and Mother Theresa's of the world who obviously weren't interested in creating a profitable company – although even they had to find ways to raise funds to support their causes. As discussed, it is *not* mandatory that your mission be directly related to what you sell or offer – but you do have to find a way to make it a distinct aspect of your brand and its operation. That means finding visible and effective ways to demonstrate its presence and your commitment to the Social Benefit you're considering.

• Fuel Type #2: Buyer Benefit
Is Buyer Benefit the type of fuel you should fill 'er up with? Ask yourself these questions:

What large, distinct advantage can I offer my clients and customers that my competition doesn't?

The type of Buyer Benefit that makes a Vehicle run the best is a major and systematic one – something integral to every single customer's experience and something that goes beyond coupons, rewards programs or other normal discount deals. For example, a dental office that converts to a luxurious spa experience (as many actually have) to mitigate the typical dental appointment's discomfort and pain with comfort and pampering. Your Buyer Benefit should be the kind of big statement that makes a consumer stand up and take notice.

Can my company realistically offer this Buyer Benefit?

Generally, adding a big Buyer Benefit to the mix will affect a business's bottom line in a negative way in the near term, due to needing some capital to put it in place (but not all Buyer Benefits do this, so if yours doesn't, go for it!). The only way to lessen the blow is if you are able to (a) charge more as a result of the benefit or (b) attract enough new customers with the new benefit to make up for the "loss leader" aspect. In either case, you may want to test the benefit with a "soft launch" just to get an idea of how it will affect your profit and loss picture.

Am I the first to offer this Buyer Benefit?

To really make the Buyer Benefit stand out, you have to be the first in your area or industry to offer it. If you're seen as copying someone who has already successfully implemented the same Buyer Benefit, it won't have the same impact, unless you find a way to boost the benefit to a greater degree in a meaningful manner. It is true, however, that duplicating a buyer benefit with your own unique spin can bring its own success – think of Target building on Kmart and Walmart's low price model and adding some style to the mix.

• Fuel Type #3: Disruptive Innovation Mission

Is a Disruptive Mission the right pick for you? Ask yourself these questions:

Is there a fundamental way I can transform the way I offer my specific products and/or services?

As an example of a Buyer Benefit mission, we mentioned a dental office that transformed itself into a spa-like environment. For a dental office to actually be *disruptive*, however, it would have to do something extreme – like, perhaps, a hygienist would actually travel to clean a patient's teeth at the patient's home or workplace. Practically speaking, this might be a stretch, but perhaps not with today's technology – who knows?

The point is, to really come up with a potent Disruptive Innovation fuel, you have to be willing to look at what's possible, rather than what's already being done. That, of course, requires some serious out-of-the-box thinking. Technology and our ability to instantly communicate on the go has opened up some serious disruptive opportunities that many businesses have already taken advantage of. Consider that as you ponder your particular Disruptive Innovation.

What obstacles are there to my proposed disruption? How formidable are they?

Generally, Disruptive Innovation will encounter some blowback down the line, because it is a serious threat to business-as-usual. In Uber's case, the company still faces many regulatory challenges, as it is basically a taxi business that operates outside the standardized, in many cases archaic and politically motivated, licensing procedure put in place by many cities. Uber knew that going in and opted to challenge those procedures as it progressed, rather than allowing them to stop Uber before it started. Luckily for the company, that approach has mostly worked out.

However, it is worth pondering the case of Aereo, another would-be disruptor. Founded by media mogul Barry Diller, Aereo's intent was to deliver live over-the-air network broadcasts to your computer or mobile device for an affordable monthly fee, eliminating the need for expensive cable or satellite TV hook-ups. After investors sunk almost $100 million into the company[54], however, the Supreme Court recently ruled Aereo's whole business model violated copyrights of the networks, completely short-circuiting the company's business model and plunging it into bankruptcy.[55]

Will my Disruptive Innovation choice matter in the marketplace?

Flooz.com was supposed to be a brand new currency you could use on the internet. Backed by $35 million in start-up funds and a splashy marketing campaign featuring Whoopi Goldberg, Flooz quickly flamed out, because nobody really saw the need for it. Webvan.com

54. Bort, Julie. " Internet Streaming TV Service Aereo Snags Another $34 Million Investment," BusinessInsider.com, January 7, 2014 http://www.businessinsider.com/aereo-snags-another-34-million-2014-1#ixzz3LVnohFZA

55. Steel, Emily. "After Supreme Court Ruling, Aereo's Rivals in TV Streaming Seize Opening, *The New York Times*, June 29, 2013

was one of the first businesses to offer home delivery of groceries – but also quickly went bust. Then there was the famous dog sock puppet which appeared in endless TV commercials, selling the joys of ordering pet food over the internet through the brand new Pets.com. That sock puppet was soon out on the street when Pets.com was quickly put to sleep by an uninterested public.

Each of these early internet start-ups was designed to disrupt – and each of them crashed and burned. Interestingly, however, Bitcoin is now a semi-successful version of Flooz, Webvan's business mission was taken over by local grocery stores as well as other online-based companies such as Amazon and Fresh Direct, and Petco.com now succeeds doing exactly what Pets.com failed at. Although Flooz, Webvan and Pets.com were pioneers in their businesses, they quickly encountered the biggest problem of being first to the party – nobody else is in the room!

Timing is *critical* to disruption – the marketplace has to be ready for it. Flooz, Webvan and Pets.com all tried too soon and paid the price. You can never know for sure when the time is right for your specific disruption, but testing your idea is always an important step to take – as is consulting with lawyers if you fear you're skirting some legal restrictions.

In short, the price of true disruption can be high – but, since the pay-off can be enormous, the gamble can be more than worth it.

ACTION STEP B: ACTIVATING YOUR VEHICLE'S GPS

If you've identified which of the three fuels best suits your Vehicle, you can now program a specific destination you want to take it in. To do that, follow these steps:

1. Restate Your Life Mission.
Your Life Mission will guide you towards the right destination if you allow it. Think about the main objectives contained in your Life Mission and what kind of impact in the real world you would like to make with them.

2. Determine What "Moon Shot" Goal You Want to Pursue

Remember your stated destination will represent *how* you're going to translate your Life Mission to a concrete objective. John F. Kennedy's original Moon Shot goal of putting a man on the moon within a decade was a response to a more abstract mission of catching up to the Russians, who badly outpaced the U.S.A. in the early days of the space race. He saw the goal of putting a man on the moon as a way to galvanize NASA and the scientific community at large into winning that race.

You may want to help with the fresh water crisis in undeveloped countries. Or advance the cause of cancer research because you lost your parents to that disease. Or you may have a gift for music with which you want to somehow serve the world. In each of these cases, unless you set your mind to a specific "Moon Shot" goal, your efforts will be scattershot and unfocused.

Your "Moon Shot" goal could involve:

- Raising a certain amount of money for a cause
- Creating a certain level of valuation for your company
- Raising your profile to a certain level in your industry that would allow you to do more, achieve more and have more resources (for example, an actor wanting to win an Oscar so he can have his pick of projects)
- Breaking a specific barrier or reaching a certain threshold in your field (for example, curing cancer, creating an entirely green business, etc.)

This part has to be your call – but it's best to be ambitious. This is a long-term goal, not a short-term one – and it should be one that *does* make you a little nervous. That will motivate you to work hard and achieve more than you ordinarily would. So…shoot for the moon!

3. Send Your Vehicle Back to the Shop

Undoubtedly, you'll have to put your Vehicle up on the lift to check out its roadworthiness for the trip you're plotting out – even if it is capable of doing what you need it do. Will some minor or major modifications do the trick? Should you consider utilizing a second Vehicle (perhaps by teaming up with a nonprofit, as Chateau La Paws did)? Or do you need to create an entirely new Vehicle to really complete your Moon

Shot? This is the time to finalize the Vehicle configuration that will work best for your mission.

ACTION STEP C: GIVE YOUR
VEHICLE A ROAD TEST

Once you've decided on a fuel and a destination for your Vehicle, it's a good idea to give it a further theoretical road test. With that in mind, we've prepared a set of six questions you can ask yourself to determine whether your destination (i.e. your Moon Shot) is really viable.

• Is it simple?

To fulfill your Moon Shot, you're going to have to get people on board to help you out. That means it should be easy to understand and explain. Like a great "elevator pitch," you should be able to convey the basic thrust of the mission in less than thirty seconds – or, even better, in a breathtaking sentence that will impress the listener. Let's go back to the original Moon Shot and imagine how JFK would have summed it all up: "We're going to put a man on the moon, and we're going to give NASA all the funding and resources it needs to accomplish that goal." That, in a nutshell, was what he planned and what captivated the nation.

So practice telling your Moon Shot to a few people you trust (both in terms of judgment and discretion – you don't want it repeated to others before you get a chance at making it work!). Make sure it garners a positive reaction from your preview audience and be open to any reasonable feedback.

• Is it sustainable?

Trying to reach your Vehicle's destination may require a fuel type that's extremely uneconomical, as we've discussed. A very ambitious Moon Shot can generate extra expenses or a drain on profits, as well as a strain on resources and personnel. So think carefully about whether the trip you want to take in your Vehicle is exponential enough to make the risk worthwhile, especially if it's going to take some time; remember you still have to support yourself and grow your business. If the initial outlook is problematic, consider the kinds of adjustments you can make that might enable it to be a doable long-term commitment.

• **Is it memorable and unique?**
An effective Moon Shot goal should be something people find compelling and out of the ordinary – a goal that people have been *wanting* a business or individual to do. While it's hard to reinvent the wheel, your overall destination should at the very least be an attention-getting place that will make potential customers, clients or supporters seriously consider working with you.

• **Is it delivering a big enough benefit?**
Another important aspect of your planning should be the benefit it actually delivers to your buyers or your cause. If it's a business benefit, then it should make a big impact in terms of money, convenience, access, price or quality of product or service. If it's a cause benefit, it should also deliver a big awareness or fundraising component (ideally both). It can also be a big *intangible* benefit – such as Chick-fil-A's public display of its values, which is attractive to those who share those values and makes them feel good about eating there.

• **Does it play into your strengths?**
If you're a technophobe who is considering a Moon Shot that requires a new and innovative mobile app or website, are you able to compensate for your lack of ability with a gifted programmer? If your goal is charity-based and you have absolutely no experience with nonprofit endeavors, are you motivated to learn enough to do it correctly? It's best if your Moon Shot goal substantially ties into your abilities and experience; if it's beyond your skill set, then, at the very least, you will need to commit to hiring the right talent to help your Vehicle reach its destination.

• **Is it part of your belief system?**
Imagine if it was suddenly revealed in the media that Chick-fil-A was secretly run by an extremist pretending to be Christian in order to boost profits? Imagine if Ben & Jerry's was secretly funded by staunch conservatives in order to make money from politically liberal consumers who would normally steer very clear of anything the conservative activists do? Both these scenarios are, of course, patently ridiculous, and equally ridiculous is *committing to a goal you don't really believe in*. If you do and the public finds out, you could at some point experience a severe backlash that could harm your business (a danger we'll discuss at more length in Chapter 11).

Having a sincere motive behind reaching your Vehicle's mission is essential. Uber's disruptive mission came from a genuine desire to provide a better cab experience, Google's famous mantra, "Don't be evil," came from the founders' desire to be better than certain old-school corporations that worshipped money over morality, and Tony Hsieh's conception of Zappos employee culture came about because of his disillusionment over how it felt to work at other companies that didn't seem to care. In each of the above cases, the company's success came from a founder's genuine desire to change things in a substantial way – to make some aspect of their business *better*. This kind of powerful emotional component that inspires a Moon Shot is often described as "fire in the belly" – and it's necessary to motivate the kind of follow through most missions require.

Of course, passion isn't enough and neither is having the right Vehicle in place. You must take targeted action through your Annual Campaigns to realize true progress – and we'll talk about that process in our next chapter.

CHAPTER 8:

YOUR ANNUAL CAMPAIGNS — FROM GOAL TO REALITY

His prospects didn't look good.

He was thrown out of college when he was caught with a female student in his dorm room. It was the 60's and that kind of thing wasn't allowed.

A couple of years later, his father who owned an billboard advertising company was overwhelmed by the debt he had incurred as a result of an expensive acquisition. He ended up tragically killing himself.

The son, who had already been working at the company, became the CEO. He proved very adept at the billboard business and steered it into more successful waters. He ended up with a virtual monopoly on it in his city.

And then he saw another business opportunity – a small local UHF television station, Channel 17, was on the block. Even though he knew nothing about the TV business, he bought it and changed its call letters to WTCG – short for "Watch This Channel Grow." Nobody knew how exactly that growth would happen; at the time, there was no cable, internet or satellite TV and viewers had to have a special additional set-top antenna to receive channels that went above 12. Even with that special antenna, UHF channels were still frequently snowy with poor picture and audio quality.

But the son had his eyes fixed on a goal far above roof aerials and above the atmosphere where TV and radio signals traveled. In fact, he had his eyes on space – and the new communication satellites that were just being launched into orbit around earth. And he saw a huge opportunity.

He began broadcasting his UHF channel over the satellite and into homes that were just getting hooked up with brand-new cable services. With this new technology, WTCG became a *national* channel – he branded it as a "Super-Station." He bought a major league baseball team, even though he knew nothing about running one – and put their games exclusively on his new Super-Station. The local franchise soon became tagged as "America's Team" and gained more exposure (and revenue) as a result.

A couple of years later, he had another idea – why not devote an entire channel to news, 24 hours a day, 7 days a week? In 1980, he put CNN up on the satellite. It was also an instant success. He then bought the ailing MGM movie studio's library of films for 1.5 billion dollars – and started a classic movie channel which he also put up on the bird.

Ted Turner, because he saw the future before anyone else, because he had a mission in place to pioneer cable TV programming, and, most importantly, because he had a strategic plan that would enable him to accomplish what no one else had ever done, built a huge media empire from virtually nothing – an empire that was finally bought out by Time Warner in 1996 for billions and billions of dollars.

It was an astounding success story. In Turner's words, "If I hadn't started the Turner Broadcasting System I couldn't have afforded to buy it. And if I hadn't started it, I would certainly not be qualified to work here in any capacity."

From the moment he bought his UHF television station, Ted Turner had a strong Life Mission in place – to use the new satellite technology to create national programming alternatives to the big networks. And he succeeded due to a series of Annual Campaigns that took him ever closer to his goal. A lowly UHF station that ran classic movies and reruns of old TV shows became the Vehicle that drove Turner to the founding of a massively successful media conglomerate that pioneered many of the cable channel formats we still watch today – all because Turner moved towards his goal methodically with an overall vision in his mind, sometimes not even knowing what the next Annual Campaign might be, but nevertheless inching step-by-step toward his goal.

If the owner of a local billboard company can become an internationally recognized media baron, what can you accomplish through the right planning process?

In this chapter, we're going to help you develop your Annual Campaigns that will advance your Vehicle towards its desired destination. Annual Campaigns are the stages you take your Vehicle through in order to translate your dreams into reality – so it's all-important you focus on making them realistic, viable but still ambitious.

In our next Action Guide, we'll focus on how to create effective and powerful Annual Campaigns. But first, we'd like to discuss at a little more length elements you need to have established in your organization in order to carry out your mission – and whatever your latest Annual Campaign happens to be.

ESSENTIAL ELEMENTS FOR
ANNUAL CAMPAIGN SUCCESS

Creating an end goal is only the starting point for an organization; putting it into action with a series of Annual Campaigns is a far more complex and tricky proposition. That's why you must lay the groundwork with your company or nonprofit by making the following essential elements a prominent part of your operation.

Essential Element #1: Make your mission
a part of your hiring process.
The wrong time to see if a hire is a fit for your organization's mission is *after* you hire that person. If new hires don't understand or care about your short and long-term goals, they won't be motivated to make that extra effort to reach them.

With that in mind, always make your mission a part of the job interview to see how receptive the person is about the organization's objectives and work culture. Your vetting process shouldn't just be about qualifications for the actual position; it should also be concerned with how enthusiastic the candidate is about what you ultimately want to accomplish.

Of course, sometimes no matter what you do, you'll still end up with an employee that doesn't work out – but, when you make Mission Screening a part of your hiring process, you cut down on the chances of that happening. And, don't forget, there are also innovative ways to weed out someone who isn't fitting in at an early stage of their training. Zappos, for example, had a policy of actually offering a four figure bonus to any new employee who wanted to quit. The company figured if the person took the money, he or she wasn't very committed in the first place!

Essential Element #2: Make your mission a part of your company culture.
In the previous chapter, we discussed how FedEx created the "Purple Promise" in order to announce its mission not only to the world, but also to its own employees. Find your own way of putting your mission front and center with your people – and make sure your philosophy is a vital part of your day-to-day operation. Also, recognize and reward those employees or volunteers who go above and beyond the call of duty in fulfilling your current Annual Campaign.

Essential Element #3: Make yourself accountable.
If you don't uphold the tenets of your mission, those you're leading will soon lose faith in it – as well as you. You must lead the charge towards your goals and always be seen as an example of your mission's best principles. Be open to feedback from those around you in order to continue to improve your performance – and further motivate your people.

Essential Element #4: Work with Outside Vendors and Partners Who Support Your Goals
Just as your employees need to be cheerleaders for your cause, so should any outside parties you work with. There almost always end up being exceptions to this rule, but, for the most part, try to work with those who want to support your mission and help you advance towards it. They'll add to the positive energy and might also contribute ideas, time or even money to helping your organization move forward.

Essential Element #5: Brand with Your Mission in Mind

Finally, the public at large needs to be aware of your mission in as powerful a way as possible. That happens through your branding and advertising. One of the main reasons to have a mission in place is to attract others to your side – but to do that, of course, they have to know about your mission. We'll discuss Mission Marketing in the very next chapter, but for now, know that your messaging should always be mission-oriented.

Now, let's move on to our next Action Guide – so you can start devising your first Annual Campaign!

ACTION GUIDE STAGE 3: FORMULATING YOUR ANNUAL CAMPAIGNS

*"As for the future, your task is not
to foresee it, but to enable it."*

~ Antoine de Saint Exupery

One Annual Campaign won't do the trick.

No, your long-range mission is achieved through a *series* of Annual Campaigns. If we view your Moon Shot as the ultimate destination of a long journey, then each Annual Campaign represents an important leg of that journey.

Each Annual Campaign should take you to an important benchmark (or perhaps several of them). As you arrive at those benchmarks, you should constantly adjust and update your future Annual Campaigns based on how much (or how little) progress you've attained on the one you just completed. While your overall mission should serve as your rock, anchoring your total organizational vision, Annual Campaigns should be seen as a much more fluid process as they are much more susceptible to real-world disruptions.

Keep in mind that Annual Campaigns can be difficult to shepherd to success; some studies show that that over 70% of change initiatives fail.[56] But frequently, that high rate of failure is more a reflection of Annual Campaigns that try to do too much at once. From the Harvard Business Review: *"In our experience, the reason for most of those failures is that in their rush to change their organizations, managers end up immersing themselves in an alphabet soup of initiatives. They lose focus...the result is that most change efforts exert a heavy toll, both human and economic."*[57]

That's why Annual Campaigns must be carefully thought out. They shouldn't take on too much at one time; instead, they should be seen as measured attainable steps to advance an organization towards its mission. And they should aim at modest and incremental changes, rather than radical upheavals.

With that in mind, this Action Guide will take you through the process of creating your own Annual Campaigns that will empower you to draw ever closer to your Mission-Driven dream.

Action Step A: Brainstorm Benchmarks
As noted, each of your Annual Campaigns should be about achieving one or more realistic benchmarks within a given calendar year, each of which is designed to take you ever closer towards fulfilling your mission.

In this first Action Step, devise a progression of the next 12 significant benchmarks you feel you need to reach in order to advance towards your ultimate goal. Again, make sure these benchmarks are realistic and attainable – but also make sure that one benchmark builds on the preceding one (For example, Ted Turner couldn't have put his TV station on the satellite – without first buying the TV station!). This list of benchmarks will most likely not take you all the way to your Moon Shot – but they should represent the most immediate goals you need to reach. 12 is enough for now and are more than enough to consider at one time in terms of your Annual Campaign considerations.

(Note: If you already began your organization with your mission in mind, you may not need as many benchmarks as someone who is retooling their company to reflect a new goal. Someone starting from

---

56. Beer, Michael and Nohria, Nitin. "Cracking the Code of Change," *Harvard Business Review*, May-June 2000 Issue
57. Beer and Nohria.

scratch must also consider creating an overall company culture that's Mission-Driven as well as reaching external objectives.)

Put your 12 benchmarks in chronological order, from first to last, as indicated here:

12 Significant Benchmarks (First to Last)

1. _____

2. _____

3. _____

4. _____

5. _____

6. _____

7. _____

8. _____

9. _____

10. _____

11. _____

12. _____

Review the list with others in (and outside of) your organization. Take in their feedback, revisit the list and revise as necessary based on the comments and criticism that makes sense to you.

Action Step B: Convert Strategy into Action

An Annual Campaign must include a systematic way of achieving your intended benchmarks. Obviously you can't wish these benchmarks into existence; you must devise concrete ways to reach them.

Before you write out your Annual Campaign for the year ahead, answer the following questions which will supply you with critical guidelines:

- **What benchmarks do I believe I can reach in the next 12 months?**

Take your list of benchmarks and begin with the first significant one. How much progress can you make towards it in the first year? What other associated benchmarks might you want to reach as well? Break them down into Internals (goals within the organization) and Externals (goals outside your organization) that serve your mission and lead you towards your goal.

- **What specific actions do I need to take to reach each benchmark?**

  Do you need to hire more personnel? Do you need to partner up with someone outside your business or nonprofit? Do you need to obtain more resources? Bolster your social media strategy? Research and mastermind what you need to actually do to reach your yearly goals.

- **What systems must I put into place?**

  Many benchmarks are only reached by certain repetitions of tasks or ongoing communication of constant messaging. For instance, one benchmark may be writing a book such as this one to create a platform for your mission; that means you may want to create a system to get so many pages done a week, so that, at the end of the year, you have an entire book written. For that kind of scenario, you should schedule a certain amount of time every week specifically for the purpose of writing those pages – and transform that writing time into a habit.

- **What timeline is best for achieving the benchmarks in question?**

  Some benchmarks can be reached in days, some in weeks, some in months. Based on what actions need to be taken and which systems need to be established, determine your best "guesstimate" on when each benchmark will be reached and create a schedule based on those forecasts.

- **How can I keep myself – and my organization accountable?**

  As your Annual Campaign progresses, you also need to have in place a method of accountability – for yourself, for those who work for you and for the organization as a whole. Unless you take stock of your progress on a regular basis with a clear and unbiased eye, you really won't be aware of how far you've come – or what you might need to adjust to make sure you stick to your Annual Campaign's schedule.

- **What obstacles will I face in trying to achieve my benchmarks?**

  Your Annual Campaign should contain contingency plans in the event negative events you can't control affect its progress. Perhaps you won't have as much money available as you thought, perhaps your industry as a whole will face structural problems, perhaps you will lose a key ally or resource. You can't plan for everything, but you can plan for common pitfalls that all organizations face.

With these answers in place, create a very *specific* Annual Campaign that spells out actionable steps that will move you towards your benchmarks throughout the year. Another great idea to help see your Annual Campaign through? Create a visualization or vision board of your benchmarks as you begin to work towards them so you (and others around you) can keep a mental picture of what you want to achieve.

Action Step C: Review and Revise
As your Annual Campaign progresses through the year, sit down every three months and review its effectiveness, through the following method:

- **Make sure your Annual Campaign is moving your organization forward at the desired rate.**
  It's generally easy to see whether a plan is working or not; either progress is being made or it isn't. If you don't make a point of following up, however, you can easily lose a lot of valuable time while your organization is spinning your wheels. That's why we suggest a quarterly review of your Annual Campaign, preferably with your staff, to keep on top of it and make changes as needed.

- **Revise Systems and Actions as Needed**
  If progress is not being made, then obviously changes need to be made to your Annual Campaign. The critical part of that process is identifying what isn't working – and not monkeying around with what *is* working.

On occasion, you will find your Annual Campaign is working for one aspect of your business – but in some other way is causing harm. For example, resources may be allocated to the Annual Campaign that are needed elsewhere for the basic operation of your company to run smoothly. This is another important area to address as you obviously have to keep your basic infrastructure healthy at all costs.

- **Change Personnel as Needed**
  You might have the wrong person tending to a critical part of your Annual Campaign. If so, you must determine whether you can

switch out that person with someone else in the organization – or replace the person all together. Hopefully, the former option will work as opposed to the latter, but, in any event, if someone cannot help the organization follow through on its Annual Campaign, that someone either needs retraining or a replacement.

- **Adjust Benchmarks if Necessary**
  While you certainly want to achieve all your goals for the year, you also may have to face reality if one or more of them become impossible for one reason or another. When that's the case, it's better to rethink your benchmarks rather than having your Annual Campaign completely crash and burn. Sometimes survival is a benchmark when you go through difficult times – so take stock of your situation when trouble arises and think how you can still achieve in the face of adversity.

That concludes our Action Guide to completing the 3 Stage process of formulating your Life Mission, customizing your Vehicle and creating your Annual Campaigns. This is by necessity a very general guide as everyone reading this book will obviously have very different parameters for their Mission-Driven efforts. Hopefully, the preceding pages have provided you with some universal principles that can direct you through the process.

But there's still more to come.

In our next few chapters, we're going to move on to a few more important aspects of what you need to know when it comes to implementing your Mission-Driven efforts. Next up – marketing, a critical part of any organization's success, especially when it comes to communicating your mission.

CHAPTER 9

MARKETING YOUR MISSION

He thought it was absolutely the most disgusting thing he had ever seen in his life.

To most people, having a mammoth company like McDonalds invest heavily in your company would be a godsend. To Steve Ells, it was a necessary evil. Although he had built his fledgling "fast-casual" restaurant chain to a modicum of success – a total of 18 locations - he needed more capital to truly create a full-fledged nationwide franchise.

The problem was that he viewed the restaurant business through a completely different prism than the Golden Arches. They wanted him to put in drive-through windows and he refused. They wanted him to serve breakfast – again, he refused. He insisted on using high-quality ingredients and they upbraided him on costs, saying that, proportionally, he spent as much on food as a classy steakhouse. That made him laugh. All he sold were burritos.

Now, McDonalds was out to school him by sending him to their chicken farm in Arkansas, where they sourced much of their poultry – and he was appalled by what he saw.

The experience cemented his business mission in his mind. He returned and told his staff he wanted to change the way the world eats. He created a Mission Statement that centered on the words, "Food with Integrity," and worked to increase their use of naturally raised meat, organic produce, and dairy without added hormones.

McDonalds thought he should at least use his efforts as a marketing wedge – the execs wanted him to put the word "fresh" in the name of his restaurants. His response? "That's a bunch of (expletive deleted). Why would we do that? It doesn't make any sense."[58]

After a few years, McDonalds realized Chipotle was not a very good match with the huge multinational and divested itself of Chipotle's stock. That was fine with Ells – by that time, his chain was up to 500 restaurants and more and more investors were clamoring for stock. But he did need to market the business in a powerfully effective way in order to keep revenues rising. So, Ells hired an established ad agency to help them make a nationwide impact with their marketing. Unfortunately, the experience was much the same as what he went through with McDonalds. He got the typical slick advertising advice, same as he got the typical fast food advice from Mickey D's. He quickly fired the agency.

Because Chipotle did food its own way, he thought the marketing should be just as unique – so he took the whole operation in-house and hired a Chief Marketing Officer to target the audience he thought was Chipotle's path to true success - millennials. Millennials believed in the kind of food sourcing principles that Ells did and would pay a little more to support those principles. But Ells had to get the Chipotle message out to them in a way that was trustworthy; millennials didn't fall for the usual traditional media marketing – they felt it was inauthentic. Ells' conundrum was that Chipotle needed *some* traditional media to reach the largest possible audience.

The answer came in the form that, ironically, was 100% millennial – YouTube.

Ells had commissioned an animated short to be created called "Back to the Start," which featured country music legend Willie Nelson singing Coldplay's song, "The Scientist," about going back to basics; the cute and appealing two-minute film focused on a farmer's journey from running a huge industrialized farming "factory," much like

58. Stock, Kyle and Wong, Venessa. "Chipotle: The Definitive Oral History," Bloomberg Businessweek, February 2, 2015.

the McDonalds one that had offended Ells, to engaging with more sustainable and humane practices. It garnered a terrific reception online and was quickly and heavily shared through social media.

That was just fine with Ells, who felt "Back to the Start" perfectly captured the Chipotle ethos. He wanted as many people to see it as possible. To that end, he thought about running the entire two-minute short during the Super Bowl – but the price for that ad placement would have been higher than the company's entire media budget for the year. Finally, they decided to run it during the Grammy ceremony in 2012 – they figured the blockbuster music telecast of the year would deliver more of their target audience anyway.

The strategy was a success. Ells continued to produce similar shorts about responsible farming and food sourcing. They were able to actually *lower* their media budget over the next few years, because their targeted marketing was so effective.

The student truly surpassed the teacher. While Chipotle is experiencing skyrocketing profits and success, expanding to over 1800 locations and topping $4 billion in sales in 2014, McDonalds' net income in 2014 fell by 14%[59] - and, as we write these words, it's been announced that the CEO, a 25-year company veteran,

is departing. Meanwhile, its "Lovin' It" marketing campaigns have been greeted with scorn in the business arena. In the words of the *Wall Street Journal*, "McDonald's looks like it's trying too hard to look trendy—and more like Chipotle, a hip chain that claims the mantle of 'food with integrity."[60]

The difference between the two companies is instructive. While Chipotle properly aligns its marketing with an authentic mission, McDonalds is flailing around with gimmicks and feel-good messaging that doesn't have much behind it. Again from the Wall Street Journal: "You can't give McDonald's a makeover…McDonald's should dump the "love" mantra and get back to the excellence mantra that made the Egg McMuffin a world-wide phenomenon."[61]

59. Bachelder, Katherine. "I'm Not Lovin' It, McDonalds," *The Wall Street Journal*, February 3, 2015.
60. Bachelder
61. Bachelder

In other words…McDonalds needs to market *its* original mission.

In this chapter, we're going to break down how Chipotle created Mission-Driven marketing campaigns that had the maximum impact for the minimum cost – and how you can put the same processes to work for you with your business.

YOUR MISSION MARKETING TARGETS

With any kind of marketing, it's important to zero in on certain targets. With Mission-Driven marketing, it's essential. When you have those targets in your sights, your marketing will allow you to bond in an authentic and powerful way with those who share your mission – a bond that has a strength that goes way beyond any conventional marketing.

If you can hit all, or even most, of the following five targets, you'll quickly attain that kind of bond.

Target #1: Your Audience

How well do you know your audience? If the answer is, "Not very well," then it's time to dig in deep and get acquainted.

Hopefully you've taken our earlier advice and chosen a mission that will appeal to your most likely buyers. This is a crucial alignment that needs to be in place. As already discussed, Chipotle did, in fact, already have a desirable target demo in mind as it moved forward with its enormous expansion: Millennials. And they made a perfect choice in that regard.

Millennials (those roughly 19 to 36 years old) act differently than their predecessors, the Baby Boomers, and many brands, like McDonalds, have been slow to understand and take advantage of that difference. Chipotle wasn't. In fact, they knew they were in the exact right place at the exact right time to meet the Millennials' specific eating preferences.

Millennials wanted to turn away from the traditional fast food giants, because of the constant downgrading of food quality to keep profit margins high and prices low – but they still needed a high-value, low-cost place to eat, and Chipotle was there to fill the bill. But, as the chain expanded to mammoth heights, marketing was required to deliver the Chipotle message to potential customers in new locations. That marketing had to continue to appeal to millennials.

According to research, there are three main strategies that work best when it comes to the millennial mindset:[62]

1. Appeal to the values that drive them: Happiness, passion, diversity, sharing and discovery.

2. Understand their realistic lifestyles and experiences and find ways to enrich that realism.

3. Make sure they feel informed and involved, not just marketed to.

Chipotle absorbed these strategies and used them to fuel their Mission-Driven marketing, as you're about to see. Understanding their target audience was the critical first step to formulating an effective marketing plan – and it should be your first step as well.

Target #2: Your Message
Here's a well-worn, but very valid proverb: It's not *what* you say, but *how* you say it. That's never truer than when it comes to crafting your mission's marketing message. Once you've established what your target demographic is and researched its mindset, the next step is to move on to crafting a marketing message that lines up with your mission as well as your demographic's tastes.

Here's how Chipotle did it. As noted, millennials scorn traditional marketing and would rather feel informed and involved. Chipotle was smart enough to acknowledge that fact and make their marketing much more about its mission than its actual food or restaurant experience. By using the "Food with Integrity" tagline, the marketing message immediately elevated the quality of its offerings in the public's eye and also cemented support for healthier farming practices. It also avoided making empty marketing promises that millennials would reject as a cliché. For example, imagine if Chipotle claimed they served "Tasty Food with Integrity" or "Delicious Food with Integrity," the kind of language most restaurants would insist on having in their advertising? It would have diluted the effect. By making the tagline a seemingly-simple declaration of fact, however, Chipotle showed *its* marketing integrity to millennials.

---

62. Spenner, Patrick. "Inside the Millennial Mind: The Do's & Don'ts of Marketing to this Powerful Generation," *Forbes Magazine*, 4/16/2014

So - how can you sum up your organizational mission in just a few words? A few words that will have the proper impact with your audience? What kind of language will work best with your target group? You may end up spending what seems like an endless amount of time putting those few words together (which you'll also want to test to see how they connect with the public), but you'll find it's worth all the blood, sweat and tears to get this part of the Mission-Driven marketing equation exactly right.

Target #3: Your Media

There's a reason you see all those bladder control commercials on TV newscasts – it's because it's the most effective way for those companies to reach older viewers, who make up the overwhelming majority of the audience for such channels as Fox News and CNN. They purposely picked media that would deliver them the biggest audience that would be receptive to their pitch.

Now that you have your target audience and messaging in place, it's time for you to do the same. The good news is, thanks to the internet, there's never been so many different options for marketers to explore in the history of mankind. When you're choosing where to deliver your message, however, it can be just as important to *avoid* certain media as it is to choose the right ones.

Case in point, Chipotle's media strategy. From the get-go, Chipotle wanted to avoid the traditional fast food TV advertising that might cause the company to be lumped in the same category as other chains it was anxious to differentiate itself from. Instead, it embarked on a low-cost high-impact strategy using primarily alternate media to connect with its target audience.

Beginning with its "Back to the Start" short, the company continued to seek out nontraditional marketing media to post its mission-oriented content, using music videos featuring Karen O of the Yeah Yeah Yeahs and Willie Nelson, another animated short called *The Scarecrow* that linked up with a mobile video game, and a four-part original internet series entitled *Farmed and Dangerous* on Hulu.com, which was a satire of "Big Food" practices. All of these videos and products featured very little actual marketing of Chipotle beyond being branded with its name – yet all strongly supported and furthered its "Food with Integrity" mission.

Perhaps more importantly, all of these projects gained Chipotle a ton of free publicity and good will on a very small budget. As Marc Crumpacker, Chipotle's Chief Marketing Officer, puts it, "We're trying to appeal to an audience we call the 'conscientious eaters.' Those people are already pretty loyal, but we're trying to resonate with people who aren't thinking about that much. They don't have to choose Chipotle, ultimately. But we'd love for them to think about where their food comes from."[63]

So think about what sort of content will best deliver your Mission-Driven message – and which media will best deliver that content to your demographic.

Target #4: Your Authenticity
Many have found marketing can be a very slippery slope when it comes to promoting a mission. Any whiff of blatant self-interest will destroy a carefully-crafted marketing strategy within seconds on social media if you're not careful.

We'll turn to our old friend McDonalds again to demonstrate this hard fact of life. The burger giant attempted to solicit heartwarming tales from its customers in 2012 by creating the Twitter hashtag, #McDStories. What followed was a torrent of abusive tweets from, you guessed it, millennials who replied harshly with these kinds of comments:

*Dude, I used to work at McDonald's. The **#McDStories** I could tell would raise your hair.*

*One time I walked into McDonalds and I could smell Type 2 diabetes floating in the air and I threw up. **#McDStories***

*These **#McDStories** never get old, kinda like a box of McDonald's 10 piece Chicken McNuggets left in the sun for a week[64]*

We don't mean to pick on McDonalds, but it's clear their marketing perspective isn't as sharp as when it knew how to sell itself like no other brand did. The fact is, it's way too easy for a business to set itself up for ridicule with botched Mission-Driven marketing – the public is just waiting to pounce.

---

63. Morrison, Maureen. "Chipotle Bucks Fast-Food Convention While It Still Can," *Advertising Age*, March 12, 2012

64. Hill, Kashmir. "#McDStories: When A Hashtag Becomes a Bashtag," *Forbes*, 1/24/12

How do you avoid that? By running a business that supports your mission's principles – and by always being consistent and truthful when marketing that mission. To do otherwise, as you'll see in the next chapter, can fatally compromise your credibility and even your entire brand.

That's why you should always expect your Mission-Driven marketing to be challenged – and you should always be ready to take on that challenge.

Chipotle actually wasn't. When it produced its "Back to the Start" video, the company viewed it as a broad-based fable of sorts, not to be applied specifically to Chipotle itself. However, since it had the Chipotle name on it, viewers viewed it as Chipotle making promises about how it sourced its food. That led to a complaint to the Better Business Bureau, who asked Chipotle to prove they practiced the processes preached in their video – and luckily, Chipotle was able to pass that test and be given the BBB stamp of approval.

Know this: If you can't back up your Mission-Driven marketing with facts, if you're exaggerating or being disingenuous in any way, you *will* take a hit down the line. The power of being Mission-Driven derives from being truthful and genuine; once you violate those principles, you're in trouble. So it's best to be aware, even if you believe you're just passing on information, you're still creating expectations about your organization. Even the Red Cross takes a lot of heat for the way it spends revenues from donations.

As Chipotle CMO Crumpacker said of the BBB experience, "One of the things we learned is to be very truthful and accurate in the things we're doing…while we think we're telling a simple story, the people watching it are taking a lot away from it, and if you're not careful they may take something away that you weren't expecting. You don't want people turning against you."[65]

Target #5: Your Community
With Mission-Driven marketing, you don't want to just talk at people – you want to talk *with* them. That means seeking out and even creating opportunities to connect with the community that supports your mission.

---

65. Morrison, Maureen. "Chipotle Leaps Forward With 'Back to the Start," *Advertising Age*, November 26, 2012

Chipotle understood this principle, as did Ben & Jerry's before them, and focused on finding ways to interact and bond with their community in fun, relevant and educational ways that weren't preachy or tedious. Instead, the intent was to create an ongoing dialogue that's both socially aware and entertaining.

For example, over the past few years, the company has held a series of free "Cultivate Festival" outdoor events that draw tens of thousands of people. The festivals hook up attendees with local unique foods and beverages under the Chipotle umbrella. It has also launched a "Cultivating Thought" program by adding printed content to its bags and cups from such high-profile writers as Toni Morrison and Malcolm Gladwell, and even cutting-edge comics such as Sarah Silverman.

Now – think about your organization's mission. How can you best reach the people who will respond to it the most strongly? What other local (or national) organizations can you team up with who also support your mission? And what interactive events and in-store (or in-office) methods can you use to further connect with your base? Remember to always try to make your mission a two-sided conversation, instead of a lecture.

WILL YOU HIT THE BULL'S-EYE?

As we hope we've made clear in this chapter, when you're moving forward with your Mission-Driven marketing, you should have a clear idea of how to present your mission in a way that will make your potential customers respond in the strongest possible way.

That means you must clearly understand every angle of your campaign, including...

- **Who you're talking to**
  Once again, know your target audience thoroughly – their behaviors, their opinions and their attitudes towards marketing.

- **What you're talking about**
  You yourself have to understand your own mission thoroughly in order to carry it out effectively - both its advantages and its disadvantages.

• What makes your mission unique

What is it about your mission that makes it different from other organizations' – and how can you best exploit that difference to make people stand up and take notice? How can you take advantage of that difference in your marketing?

• Why your mission matters

You have to sell your mission to your audience – which means you have to understand what makes it important to *them*. Chipotle, for example, continually promotes the fact that their food-sourcing improves their menu items' quality and adds extra value to their meals (which makes the slightly-higher prices justifiable).

• What makes your mission authentic

How is your mission reflected in how you do business? Is there any aspect of your business that undercuts that mission? If so, how do you account for that? This is an issue you MUST resolve before engaging in Mission-Driven marketing.

• Why Mission-Driven marketing may not be enough

While Mission-Driven marketing certainly packs a punch, you may also need to do more traditional hard-sell tactics to support your organization. This is a fact of life even Chipotle has to face. Of Chipotle's non-traditional marketing strategy, restaurant marketing veteran Dan Dahlen says, "Chipotle will eventually get to that point, that to drive same-store sales they'll have to go to TV. As you get into the top spenders in the category, there's a correlation between share of voice and share of stomach."[66]

Even Chipotle's CMO realizes that day is coming – but the company is putting it off for as long as possible. "The alternative is to switch to the type of marketing that every other fast-food company uses - with these new menu items and big ad campaigns to promote them. Once you get on that model, I think it's very, very hard to get off. I want to try to do this as long as I can."[67] So far, Chipotle's level of success is so huge, it's far from a pressing issue.

The rules for Mission-Driven Marketing are a little different for nonprofits – and we'll discuss that difference in the next chapter.

---

66. Morrison, Maureen. "Chipotle Bucks Fast-Food Convention While It Still Can"
67. Morrison

CHAPTER 10

MARKETING YOUR NONPROFIT MISSION

The boy wanted to be an astronaut.

His parents didn't think that was too practical a dream. His father was a doctor and both mom and dad thought that becoming an M.D. would be the perfect occupation for their son, who had already shown a bent towards science.

Unfortunately for them, the science he was drawn to was space exploration. At the age of 8, he began giving lectures on space to family and friends. At the age of 12, he won first place in a rocket design contest for his launch system that was able to put three rockets into the air at once. After being accepted at MIT, he co-founded a student organization dedicated to the exploration and development of space S.E.D.S. (Students for the Exploration and Development of Space).

But, even though throughout his undergraduate years at MIT his passion was space, his parents prevailed - and he entered Harvard Medical School in order to become an M.D. The fact was that the U.S. was winding down NASA's budget and missions and, at this point, a career devoted to space exploration didn't look remotely practical.

Still, the dream wouldn't let go of him.

During his second year of medical school, he co-founded a foundation to promote space-related projects and programs outside of the government's fading attempts. During his final year, he became CEO of a microsatellite launch company. He suddenly felt a new movement brewing that held potential for space programs backed by the private sector. He put his medical degree on hold while he returned to MIT to get a master's degree in aeronautics and astronautics; he then returned and received his medical degree from Harvard.

When all was said and done, however, his heart remained in space. Still feeling frustrated that manned space travel was more and more being relegated to history, he thought long and hard about how to motivate the kind of technological innovation that would once again get people excited about space travel.

Then one night, he read a book.

It was Charles Lindbergh's *The Spirit of St. Louis*, in which the world-famous aviator described his famous nonstop historic journey from New York to Paris in a single-engine plane – an event that transfixed the world and made it see the real possibilities of flight for the first time. But it wasn't Lindbergh's journey that struck the man that night.

No, it was what motivated Lindbergh to make the journey in the first place.

A New York hotel owner who had emigrated from France was anxious to strengthen ties between his home country and his adopted one. So he offered a prize of $25,000 to anyone who could fly from New York to Paris, which was at that time twice the distance of the longest nonstop flight. Nine teams spent a total of $400,000 to claim the $25,000 prize, with Lindbergh being the winner – with the result that "Lucky Lindy" became the hugest celebrity of the time and aviation was suddenly thought of in a whole new light.

So...if a cash prize worked that well for airplanes, why couldn't it work for rocket ships?

Peter Diamandis put down the book and decided to award $10 million to whoever could create a "suborbital, private, fully reusable spaceship." He called it the XPRIZE, with the "X" serving as a placeholder for whatever individual or company would end up sponsoring the prize.

Unfortunately, he couldn't find a sponsor - so the name "XPRIZE" just stuck.

Potential donor after donor turned him down even after he had announced the competition. People wanted to know why NASA wasn't involved and, besides, what if somebody got killed trying to do this? Everyone told him to give up.

He didn't. And finally, eight years later, he found his financial backing from the Ansari family, who had been successful in the telecommunications industry. Twenty six teams ended up competing for the money and, in 2004, aerospace engineer Burt Rutan sent a spacecraft to 100 kilometers altitude twice in two weeks, fulfilling the requirements to win the prize. The winning entry, SpaceShipOne, is now hanging in the Smithsonian Air & Space Museum – right next to the Spirit of St. Louis.

Let's start with a fairly obvious statement: Every nonprofit is a mission-based organization, whether that mission is to cure a disease, improve the environment, assist those in poverty, etc. A mission is a nonprofit's reason for existence. However, since *each* nonprofit has a mission, it's hard for them to differentiate themselves from each other *on the basis of mission alone*.

As we've discussed, that's not the case with a business that has a mission built into its operational DNA. Since most companies don't, a mission-driven business is able to stand apart in the marketplace - having a known worthy goal elevates it above those that seemingly only have a profit motive.

The nonprofit with a worthy goal, however, is one of over a million and a half other nonprofits in the U.S. alone – and all of *those* nonprofits have worthy goals as well. That means the nonprofit has a far more daunting challenge in terms of selling its specific mission to the public. They must strive to stand above and apart from all of the other nonprofits competing against each other for the same donor funds. To do this requires brand positioning, an effective and compelling story, and the ability to market your story just as effectively as the best for profit companies.

Think about your own experience with charities. You almost certainly get regular email, direct mail, social media and phone solicitations asking you to contribute to one cause or another. And you probably can't help occasionally dismissing some of them as, "Oh, it's just another charity wanting my money," even though their cause is almost certainly a good one. When you're inundated with donation requests, though, the power of each individual cause suddenly seems diminished. So the question becomes – if the organizational mission is not enough, how does a nonprofit effectively attract donors and supporters?

The answer is actually pretty simple: Just as businesses need missions to differentiate their marketing, nonprofits need brand positioning, and marketing to differentiate their mission by telling their story in a compelling way.

Peter Brinckerhoff, the author of *Mission-Based Marketing: Positioning Your Not-for-Profit in an Increasingly Competitive World*, lists the following characteristics as being essential to a successful nonprofit:

- A viable mission statement
- Ethical, accountable and transparent
- A businesslike board
- Strong, well-educated staff
- Embrace technology for mission
- Social Entrepreneurs
- A bias for marketing
- Financially Empowered
- A Vision for where you are going
- Tight Controls

Now…of that list, Brinckerhoff underlines one of the above items to indicate its prime importance. That item is *"A bias for marketing."*

Peter Diamandis, the genius behind the XPRIZE, understood that importance. He knew space travel had virtually disappeared as a goal in modern society; therefore he needed a way to (a) motivate the engineering sector that was secretly yearning for a shot at space, and (b) capture the imagination of a public that had all but given up on progressing spaceflight past the NASA era. He found that way by duplicating the contest that resulted in the historic flight of The Spirit of St. Louis - the perfect template for this modern-day equivalent as well as a marketing home run. He has continued to do that through additional XPRIZEs, like the Google Lunar Landing XPRIZE, the Global Learning XPRIZE, the Wendy Schmidt Ocean Health XPRIZE, and many others. And, to be honest, the authors of this book became such a fan of the XPRIZE that we joined its Innovation Board!

However, there are other ways a nonprofit can hit that kind of home run – ways that *don't* involve millions of dollars. Let's talk about how to accomplish that in more detail.

THE NONPROFIT MARKETING "BUCKET LIST"

At the beginning of 2014, the ALS Association was one of those nonprofits whose mission didn't attract a wide base of donors. ALS, also known as Lou Gehrig's disease (named for the beloved Yankees first baseman who contracted the disease while still an active player), had to rely on a well-worn network of contributors that was contracting rather than growing. In the words of Lance Slaughter, head of fundraising for the organization, "It's very difficult to fundraise because most people have never heard of ALS and it's a very complex disease to discuss and explain."

In 2014, however, a freak social media stunt suddenly added an extra $100 million to the ALS coffers – all within the space of 30 days.

The Ice Bucket Challenge – in which someone dumps a bucket of ice water over his or her head and challenges someone else to do the same in order to promote a cause – became a viral sensation in August of 2014. It was originally a stunt done among pro golfers to promote their pet charities. One golfer, however, made it specific to ALS – and challenged his cousin, whose husband suffered from ALS, to do the Challenge. It went viral in the town where the cousin lived and spread quickly from there, to the point where it became a must-do for celebrities as varied as Kate Upton, Benedict Cumberbatch, Martha Stewart and LeBron James.

What's interesting is that, even though the Ice Bucket Challenge and the XPRIZE competition were both hugely successful, their origins couldn't be more different. While the XPRIZE marketing maneuver was consciously conceived and executed by Diamandis, the Ice Bucket Challenge was a "happy accident" in which a popular fundraising tool for multiple charities suddenly became a single-charity phenomenon that brought enormous rewards to the ALS Association - without that organization really having to do much to create that outcome. It was also an example of what happens when a social media marketing plan goes viral.

The truth is any nonprofit marketing maneuver's effectiveness will depend, as with most things in life, on a combination of solid, smart planning and a large dose of luck. Since the latter can't be controlled, we're going to focus on the former – and offer a "Bucket List" of five factors any nonprofit should try to incorporate in any sort of high-profile marketing campaign.

• Engagement

One thing that both the Ice Bucket Challenge and the XPRIZE competition had in common was a high degree of engagement. The Challenge was something fun and out of the ordinary that anyone could do – and, more importantly, anyone could be challenged by a friend or relative to do. It was a natural for social media participation.

Your campaign, either through its messaging or its mechanics, must also find a way to create a strong positive response in your audience that will inspire it to become a part of your efforts in at least some small way.

• Targeting

A nonprofit campaign, just like a business campaign, must appeal to the right crowd. The XPRIZE laid down a gauntlet with its $10 million dollar prize; it was a signal that this foundation was serious about getting space exploration (excuse the pun) off the ground again - and in reawakening that passion in both engineers and that section of the general public who were anxious to see today's technology put to work to create a new kind of spacecraft.

You obviously want to find the best way of reaching those who will care the most about your specific nonprofit mission. The Ice Bucket

Challenge, for example, hooked into people who genuinely enjoy giving to charity, and who then dared other like-minded friends and family members to do the same. Depending on who you need to reach, you can use schools, social media, conventional advertising, a specific business network or any number of channels to target your desired audience.

• Building

The problem with the Ice Bucket Challenge is that it was a short-term phenomenon. Sure, 2014 was a banner year for the ALS Association, but what about 2015? Can the organization find a way to duplicate at least part of the Challenge's success in the years to come?

In contrast, the XPRIZE competition laid the groundwork for Diamandis to put together a powerful network of successful businesspeople and innovators such as Richard Branson and Paul Allen, as well as establish other foundations also designed to push technological boundaries.

When a nonprofit is putting a lot of time, effort and resources into a marketing campaign, it should do so with a larger end game in mind. Michael R. Maude, President of Partners in Philanthropy makes a distinction between marketing and development and argues the latter is more important. In his words, "Development is the process not-for-profit organizations use to secure financial support and advance their missions. It involves a transaction between a donor and an institution that is based on intangibles, like faith and trust."

Marketing should trigger development, in terms of cementing donor loyalties and growing the organization's influence. This empowers long-range growth and future marketing efforts.

• Partnering

Whenever a nonprofit can create an alliance with a more powerful (and appropriate) partner, it can't help but benefit. The Ice Bucket Challenge, again through no action on the ALS Association's part, ended up with many companies and high-profile people signing on, giving it even more of a snowball effect on social media. We've also noted how Peter Diamandis was able to tap into the network of some very prominent business people to build on his original XPRIZE initiative.

A powerful partnership can give nonprofits a bigger audience and more marketing resources than they have access to on their own – and most companies are more than happy to make these partnerships, because it gives them the appearance (and benefits) of being mission-driven. Again, the partnership should be an appropriate one, or it could dilute the nonprofit's integrity and undercut its mission. An organization trying to save the marshlands might not want to team up with the BP Corporation, for example, after its epic oil spill in the Gulf of Mexico a few years ago.

• StorySelling™

Of course, we're big advocates of using StorySelling™ - you might say we wrote the book on it (which we did…just check Amazon!) – in any marketing campaign. When you effectively tell a compelling story, the listener is more attracted to your cause and also feels more bonded to your organization. Peter Diamandis created his own winning narrative with his $10 million XPRIZE and attracted many long-term supporters with his boldness and creativity. When your organization can craft that kind of powerful story that directly relates to your mission, you'll find yourself hitting the sweet spot when it comes to the development aspect of your marketing.

NONPROFIT MISSION MARKETING MISTAKES

The above "Bucket List" items should strongly feature in your plans. But – you should also beware of some common dangers unique to nonprofits.

For example, can you imagine people turning against a nonprofit whose stated mission was to inspire and empower cancer survivors and their families? A nonprofit that had no scandal or irregularities in its operation at all? It happened – despite one of the most brilliant nonprofit marketing campaigns ever designed.

Pro basketball players used to wear what were called "ballers" – wristbands that identified them. The president of Nike thought it might be a great way to promote an athlete's new charity. Nike manufactured 5 million of them and planned to sell them for one dollar apiece to reach the nonprofit's fundraising goals. The athlete wasn't high on the idea – in his words, "When I heard that Nike was making 5 million of them, I was a little skeptical. I figured we'd be shooting them at each other for years."

He was right in one respect. They didn't sell 5 million bracelets – they ended up selling 80 million.

As you might have guessed, the athlete we're talking about is Lance Armstrong – and the charity was the Lance Armstrong Foundation.

In the wake of Armstrong's doping scandal, the Foundation, which again had done no wrong, found donations plummeting. The nonprofit was eventually forced to remove Armstrong's name and rebrand themselves as the Livestrong Foundation. Not only that, but Nike cut all ties with the organization in 2014 and stopped manufacturing the iconic yellow wristbands that made the charity a viral sensation.

As will be discussed in the next chapter, when an organization's own mission is undercut, even by external circumstances, it can take a huge hit that can threaten its very existence. So, before you move ahead with your campaign, ask yourself the following questions to avoid some serious mistakes.

Are you thinking short-term at the cost of the organization's long-term vision?

When you ignore – or worse, work against – your nonprofit's basic mission, you begin to lose the base that supports you through thick and thin. Remember, your mission defines you – and you must keep it front and center in your plans. Partnering up with an inappropriate sponsor, creating silly or disconnected messaging, and being needlessly offensive to get attention are all common ways a nonprofit can alienate dedicated donors as well as drive away potential new ones.

Do you actually have the resources to pull off what you're planning?

Marketing can be cash intensive and often consumes 35 to 50 percent of the proceeds it brings in to a nonprofit. That's the kind of spending that can make donors question where exactly their money is going. Additionally, if you rely too heavily on staffers to pull off a campaign, you take away needed bodies from the day-to-day management of the organization. There's nothing wrong with thinking big – but find alternative ways or suitable sponsors or partners to enable and empower your supersized efforts.

Is your messaging authentic?

People are skeptical of marketing in general – and many even distrust nonprofits in terms of how they're run and how much money actually is applied to the causes they represent. If your campaign is too slick and showy, it may put off those who think you're all about flash and cash rather than actually helping anyone. The Ice Bucket Challenge, in contrast, was all about real people doing a real thing and showcased in homemade videos – it's hard to get more authentic than that.

Are you showing the faces of those you're helping?

Some aspect of your campaign should showcase individuals that your organization has helped or is trying to help. The Ice Bucket Challenge became permanently attached to the ALS Foundation because a community was trying to support the wife of an ALS patient. A big part of StorySelling™ is telling your story in human terms – the more you can focus on individuals rather than a large abstract idea, the more you're going to connect with potential supporters. And here's the proof: In 2013, more than 60% of those asked said they felt most invested in a cause when the nonprofit shared a compelling story about the people it helps.

Is your board on board with your campaign plans?

One of the worst things that can happen during a major marketing effort is to have a public spat erupt when one of more board members openly criticizes that effort. The media loves controversy and, given the chance, will jump at it to report on this kind of conflict. Make sure everybody agrees with the direction of the campaign and all concerns are at least addressed to the satisfaction of all behind closed doors.

There's no question nonprofits have been in a difficult position since the Wall Street meltdown of 2008. In 2013, 80% of nonprofits reported an increase in demand for services, the 6th straight year of increased demand – and 56% were unable to meet that demand. A nonprofit's ability to successfully market their mission is more important than ever. The information in this chapter does not guarantee you'll succeed in your efforts – but it will certainly raise the odds in your favor.

CHAPTER 11

SAFEGUARDING YOUR MISSION

A study pegged him as the 23rd most trustworthy person in the nation.

Which was good, because he needed to be trustworthy. Every weeknight, he spent the better part of a half hour telling an audience of 19 million people the events of the day. Without that belief in his honesty and integrity in place…well, who would listen to him?

A large part of his credibility came from reporting out in the field, sometimes in the middle of very dangerous situations. In 2003, when the U.S. invaded Iraq, he was there, reporting that the helicopter in front of the one he rode in was hit with an RPG (rocket-powered grenade). Then, in 2005, when the devastating Hurricane Katrina struck New Orleans with an unprecedented force, he went to the scene of the disaster – and he and his network won a Peabody Award for their "Excellence in Reporting" as a result.

After ten years serving as network anchor, he had become the dominant news person on the air as well as the face of the network's news operation. He was a popular guest on late-night talk shows and had even hosted Saturday Night Live. He was well-known and well-liked. And because of his proven success, towards the end of 2014, he was given a new five-year contract, reportedly paying him $10 million a year. He was clearly at the top of his game.

But, just a few weeks later, all that would change.

On January 30th, 2015, Brian Williams paid tribute to a veteran on the NBC Nightly News, saying the man had helped protect him when the helicopter Williams was in was hit by an RPG. When that was posted on Facebook, another veteran commented, "Sorry dude, I don't remember you being on my aircraft. I do remember you walking up about an hour after we had landed to ask me what had happened." The military newspaper *Stars and Stripes* reported on the comment and soon there was talk everywhere that Brian Williams had exaggerated the incident and put himself in a damaged helicopter, when he was in fact riding in a different one.

It didn't take long for Williams to note the controversy and understand that it had to be addressed. On February 4th, he formally apologized for his mistake both on Facebook and on the nightly news, saying it was the "fog of memory" that had caused him to "conflate" the two helicopters.

He had hoped that would be the end – but, in reality, it was only just the beginning.

Soon, a clip from two years earlier of Williams on the David Letterman Show began popping up on Facebook and Twitter – a clip in which he described in dramatic detail what happened when the helicopter he was riding in was hit by enemy fire, a story that wasn't true. That raised more questions and the media began poking around at other of his claims over the years. Suddenly, his reporting on Katrina was rendered suspicious, as were his remarks about being at the Berlin Wall when it came down or about being embedded with Seal Team 6 on top secret missions.

The more people pulled on this particular thread, the more things began to unravel.

A few days later, when the firestorm hadn't cooled down, the media reported that NBC was conducting an internal review in which even his expense accounts were being questioned. Meanwhile, sarcastic memes began appearing everywhere on the internet, where doctored photos showed Williams at Iwo Jima in World War II, standing next to Dean Martin in a photo of Frank Sinatra's Ratpack, standing on the moon next to the Apollo 11 lunar module.

On January 30th, Brian Williams was the 23rd most trusted person in America. On February 9th? He was down to the 835th.[68] And one day later, on February 10th, NBC announced it was suspending Brian Williams for 6 months – without pay.

Many media commentators speculated that he would never return.

In 1985, NBC News decided to abandon synthesized music for its music and use not only a real orchestra, but also an esteemed composer. It took two years to negotiate a deal with John Williams, the famed scorer of *Star Wars, Jaws*, and *Superman,* but network executives were thrilled with the results. The theme continues to be used 30 years later in all their news programming.

The musical piece's name? *The Mission.*

That's not a coincidence. News gathering, whether it's for print, television, radio or internet, is by definition heavily Mission-Driven. Its specific mission requires the organization behind it to maintain the highest standards of journalism and integrity, or the public will quickly turn its back on it. That's why, when a reporter plagiarizes, exaggerates or misleads on a news story, a company must take swift action against the person involved or face its credibility being destroyed. When someone in as prestigious a position as Brian Williams is caught stretching the truth, the fall is fast and hard. As of the writing of this book, he has been relegated to a lesser news channel and his future is very uncertain.

In this chapter, we're going to examine why a successful Mission-Driven business is so vulnerable when a crucial misstep happens – and we'll also point out the ways you can best protect its image and its momentum when the worst does happen. By staying smart and staying focused, it's easy to avoid and deal with giant pitfalls – so you can continue reaping the enormous rewards only a Mission-Driven business can realize.

---

68. Steel, Emily and Somaiya, Ravi. "Brian Williams Loses Lofty Spot on a Trustworthiness Scale," The New York Times, February 9th, 2015

THE IMPACT OF MISSION FAILURE

As we've noted repeatedly in this book, the advantages of being successfully mission-driven are myriad and powerful; when people believe in what you're doing, they will reward you with a loyalty that goes beyond what usually accompanies simply providing a good product or service.

This, however, also leads to one deep downside for the Mission-Driven organization or even, as evidenced by Brian Williams, the Mission-Driven individual. When you are seen to betray the mission that so many entrust you with, the anger and rejection can be swift, brutal and overwhelming. Because you are connected to the public on a higher level that supersedes "business as usual," you are also held to a higher standard of conduct.

Take the example of another Mission-Driven public personality who also suffered a huge drop in popularity just a few months before Brian Williams – Bill Cosby. After a wide-ranging and lengthy pattern of sexual assault accusations by over 30 women, a great deal of heated outrage was aimed at this once-beloved comedian. Why? In the words of The Los Angeles Times:

"...the media, mainstream and social, churned with shock, acrimony and questions about Cosby's legacy. Many have taken to Twitter and other outlets to share very strong opinions, parse old Cosby jokes or analyze his behavior in recent interviews. Others simply struggle with the disorienting, though increasingly familiar, fog of anger, sorrow, disgust and, in some cases, bitter glee that settles over conversations of any scandal involving a celebrity. These dynamics are only exacerbated this time around by the personal attachment many hold for Bill Cosby.

For at least two generations, he served as a national father figure. He gave us the raggedy childhood insights of Fat Albert and later the benign patriarchy of Cliff Huxtable, who was the kind of father many Americans, of any race, wished they'd had. His groundbreaking career made him a civil rights and social activist, a role he embraced."[69]

---

69. McNamara, Mary. "In Bill Cosby Saga, Feelings of Betrayal and Vague Complicity," *The Los Angeles Times*, November 21st, 2014.

That last paragraph details the many pro-social "missions" that Cosby came to represent in the public's mind. What's interesting is Cosby's Mission-Driven image had become so powerful that even though many of these accusations surfaced as long ago as 2005, it took almost a decade for them to finally pierce the powerful armor of the public persona that he had built over a half a century. But when it did happen, it again happened fast – NBC cancelled a sitcom he had in development, TV Land and other retro channels stopped airing reruns of his older shows and many venues immediately cancelled his stand-up appearances.

What happened to Williams and Cosby can easily happen to a Mission-Driven business, should mission failure occur. When a company builds its reputation and customer base on certain principles – and then it's found to betray those principles – it can collapse just as quickly as the careers of these two seemingly-untouchable celebrities and create just as much damage.

Research verifies the catastrophic results that can occur when a brand seemingly betrays that loyalty. Economic reporter Brad Tuttle puts it this way: "Experts who study marketing and company-consumer relationships believe that brands that have developed cult-like followings for supposedly doing things the right and honorable way— Chipotle and Whole Foods come to mind—are likely to feel greater backlash if and when they appear to violate customers' trust."[70] Tuttle goes on to make the point that consumers expect the worst from monolithic businesses such as banks and cable companies – which is why they expect so much more from Mission-Driven ones.

One Mission-Driven business that has flirted uncomfortably close with mission failure in recent months is Uber, the same business we profiled back in Chapter 5. Among the accusations that have been leveled at the company are:

- Threatening to investigate the private lives of journalists who write critical pieces about the company
- Employing less-than-safe or less-than-savory drivers

---

70. Tuttle, Brad. "Why JetBlue Can Break Your Heart, but Comcast Never Will," Time.com, November 20th, 2014. http://time.com/money/3598108/jetblue-baggage-fees-betrayal-comcast/

- Invading the privacy of users of the service
- Using hardball tactics to threaten competing services

How do all these less-than-admirable tactics threaten Uber's mission – which is simply to get people to their destinations? *The New York Times* answers that question very effectively - "Uber and its investors believe that the company's long-term mission is to reinvent transportation, to become not just a taxi service but also a replacement for private cars. That mission can be realized only if people trust the company implicitly and automatically."[71]

POWERING PAST THE PITFALLS
OF MISSION-DRIVEN BUSINESSES

What does it take to really sink a Mission-Driven business – or, at the very least, substantially diminish its success? Let's look at five big pitfalls that too often threaten companies that promote their purposes – and how to ensure you survive them.

• Pitfall #1: Changing the Mission at the Expense of Your Customer

It may be impossible to believe now, but there was a brief moment in 2011 when streaming powerhouse Netflix looked as though it was a goner, due to an almost-fatal self-inflicted wound.

Netflix had basically bankrupted Blockbuster by making movie rentals by mail easy, automatic and affordable – no late fees and no late-night trips to the store to make a return. At the same time, Netflix had its eyes on the future; they didn't want to get blindsided by technology the way Blockbuster had, so they started a streaming service which DVD subscribers received as part of their monthly fee. It took off quickly. In 2010, within a matter of months, the company went from being the postal service's number one customer to becoming the biggest source of internet traffic. They correctly saw that streaming was where their business would ultimately end up and, in October 2011, they announced they were spinning off their DVD service into a separate company so they could purely focus on their internet offerings.

---

71. Manjoo, Farhad. "Uber, a Start-Up Going So Fast It Could Miss a Turn," *The New York Times*, November 18th, 2014.

What seemed like a sound business decision felt like betrayal by its customers, who suddenly had to pay almost twice as much for the same DVD/streaming combo package they had had in the past. Result? Netflix lost a million customers within a month, its stock price fell by 19%, and it had to announce in November of 2011 that at the end of 2012, over a full year away, the company would still be unprofitable.[72]

The fact is that, even though changing up its strategy was the smart move, the abrupt left turn was too much for its customers to handle at once. The company ended up reversing course a month later and cancelled plans to spin off the DVD rentals into a separate enterprise. Subscriber anger cooled and soon, the company roared back stronger than ever.

How to Power Past this Pitfall

There's certainly *more* long-term danger in not changing up a business mission when necessary. Netflix had only to look at the ruins of Blockbuster to see what happened when you failed to keep up with technology in the marketplace. But Netflix was too anxious to avoid the mistakes of its predecessor – it not only abandoned its core business too quickly, it also made the mistake of increasing the cost of the service its customers were getting by an alarming 67%. None of the temporary and traumatic losses Netflix suffered were necessary – they just tried to do too much too soon.

Instead, when you are in the midst of changing missions, make it a lengthy transition – and make your customer base feel as little of the pain as possible. Don't inconvenience them or overcharge them for a changeover that's your responsibility to pull off – or they'll resent you for making your problem *their* problem. And if you too do too much too fast, take a page from Netflix's playbook, reverse course and make amends to your customers.

• Pitfall #2: Pursuing an Outdated Mission

This was the pitfall Netflix was trying to avoid when it ran into the other one instead – that's because this one can mean a complete dead-end for your company. Times change, cultures change, and technology changes – and if your organizational mission doesn't change as well,

---

72. Pepitone, Julianne. "Netflix will lose money for all of 2012," CNN Money, November 22, 2011. http://money.cnn.com/2011/11/22/technology/netflix_unprofitable/

what brought you huge success in the past might bring you nothing but misery in the future. Remember that in 1976, Kodak owned 90% of the photography market – and in 2012, it filed for bankruptcy.[73]

What happened in between was the introduction of digital technology that made the buying and processing of camera film completely unnecessary.

How to Power Past this Pitfall

Both Blockbuster and Kodak had many opportunities to adapt to changing times – but both did too little too late. When a company owns a certain sector of an industry, it all too easily can fall into complacency, believing its dominance will weather any storm.

That's why it's important to continually analyze your business mission in terms of changing times – and ask questions such as:

- *Is our mission still relevant?*
- *Is the marketplace changing in such a way as to render us obsolete?*
- *Are consumers beginning to view us as old-fashioned and out of step?*
- *Is someone else fulfilling our mission in a newer, more efficient and/or more exciting way?*

One needs only to look at the contrasting examples of Apple and Microsoft to see how two huge Mission-Driven companies can respond to these questions quite differently – and achieve quite different results. While Apple easily morphed from being primarily a computer company to a music company to a smartphone company, all while keeping their mission solidly in place, Microsoft remains anchored to its Windows operating system as well as its Office software. While it's taken a stab at creating its own versions of music players, smartphones, video game consoles, etc., it frankly hasn't gotten very far from where it started. And, let's remember, even Windows was a direct "borrowing" of Apple's original Macintosh operating system.

---

73. Rees, Jasper. "The End of Our Kodak Moment," *The Telegraph*, January 19, 2012.

Continually updating and evolving your mission is a necessity, not an option. If your mission isn't moving forward, it's probably falling behind.

• Pitfall #3: Diluting Your Mission

JetBlue was founded in 1998 with a very distinct mission in place. That mission was, in the words of founder David Neeleman, "to bring humanity back to air travel," and was fulfilled by charging less than the big airlines but, at the same time, offering such extra amenities as a TV at every seat. It became so successful that other airlines tried (and failed) to emulate it.

However, after a few years, JetBlue ran up against some strong headwinds from the marketplace. As other airlines' began to see their profits soar, JetBlue's remained stagnant. Wall Street analysts began attacking the CEO as being "overly concerned' with passengers and their comfort, which they feel, has come at the expense of shareholders."[74] The new CEO, *not* overly concerned that the airline built its brand on a customer-friendly philosophy, began adding more seats to planes, increasing crowding, and charging more for snacks and luggage, increasing the expense to its fliers.

That, of course, upset those customers who were faithful to the company because of its mission. As CNN Money put it, "…it's clear that the values originally embraced by the brand have changed as well. For the people who loved and were loyal to JetBlue specifically because of its egalitarian, customers-first approach, the latest moves serve as a big slap in the face."[75]

The company, at least in its press releases, remains committed to a customer-first approach. Its current president claims that "JetBlue's core mission to Inspire Humanity and its differentiated model of serving underserved customers remain unchanged." But, while fliers can still enjoy that TV at their seat, many who once swore by the airline will now undoubtedly shop around for the best-priced ticket instead of the most convenient JetBlue flight.

---

74. Sanati, Cyrus. "JetBlue will need to fight for its soul against Wall Street,"
  Fortune Magazine, September 2, 2014
75. Tuttle

How to Power Past this Pitfall

Perhaps JetBlue did have to make those tweaks to its business in order to keep the company healthy. But it could have found other ways to deal with the situation rather than just announce it was still committed to its original mission and then demonstrate the opposite. There are few things worse than talking incessantly about your mission at the same time you're scaling back on it; all the trust you took so much time

building with your fan base is immediately eroded. That's because actions speak louder than words – and when the actions directly contradict the words, your public image takes a big hit.

So what should JetBlue have done?

First of all, it should have been honest about why it was doing what it was doing, instead of pretending its mission was still firmly in place. Instead of trumpeting its concern for its passengers, JetBlue should have said it was regretful that these moves were necessary.

Second of all, JetBlue should have found some ways to sweeten customer experience in more cost-effective ways. Maybe a free snack or additional loyalty program bonuses – something that would have been a significant gesture of good will to frequent customers who would feel the pain of the economizing.

Finally, they should have heeded a piece of advice we offered earlier in this chapter: *Don't change too quickly.* Rather than do a whole bunch of things that significantly detract from the fliers' experience, maybe just do one at a time over a longer period. When everything gets bad at once, people really stand up and take notice – and immediately come to the conclusion that everything about your business is going south.

• Pitfall #4: Violating Your Customers' Values

In 1998, Lululemon was founded to provide upscale yoga-fitness apparel for women. The company was a huge success and, a few years later, it was earning over a billion dollars in revenue. However, its founder, Chip Wilson, generated a lot of controversy with his outspoken ways. For example, he stated that he named the company "Lululemon" because it was hard for Japanese people to say, so they would have to make an extra effort when marketing it in their country.

"It's funny to watch them try and say it," explained Wilson. He also talked approvingly about child labor in developing countries and claimed that birth control pills led to high divorce rates.[76]

He really began to get in trouble when he said his company doesn't make clothes for plus-size women because it costs too much money. And he also blamed excessive pilling in Lululemon pants on that segment of the buying public as well, saying "Frankly some women's bodies just don't actually work for it…it's really about the rubbing through the thighs, how much pressure is there over a period of time, how much they use it."[77]

The remarks in the above paragraph caused the company's stock value to plummet by a third – and forced Wilson to resign as Lululemon CEO.

Now, none of what Wilson said had anything to do with the company's actual business practices, products or fulfillment of its stated mission. But what his remarks did do is *offend* the sensibilities of his main target group – women. He violated their values loudly and without restraint and caused tremendous damage to the brand.

How to Power Past this Pitfall

An organization's management must be careful with public remarks and their own personal actions. If a representative of a company says or does the wrong thing, it immediately causes negative repercussions throughout social media. In 2012, Mitt Romney made some infamous remarks at a private fundraiser about 47% of the American public not paying income taxes and living off the government – and how he wasn't even going to try for their votes. Someone secretly recorded the speech and it blew up all over Facebook and Twitter. And, when you write off almost half of the voters in America, you're bound to run into trouble when the November election arrives. And, in fact, it was a mistake that heavily contributed to Romney's defeat.

That's why *control* is so important to a Mission-Driven business. It has to be careful who it hires, which vendors it does business with and

---

76. Deveau, Catherine. "Yoga Mogul Has Critics in a Knot," *The Tyee*, February 17th, 2005. http://thetyee.ca/News/2005/02/17/LuluCritics/

77. Peterson, Hayley. "8 Outrageous Remarks By Lululemon Founder Chip Wilson," Business Insider, December 10, 2013. http://www.businessinsider.com/outrageous-remarks-by-lululemon-founder-chip-wilson-2013-12#ixzz3St0QezIk

what its own leaders say and do, both behind closed doors and in the public spotlight.

When this kind of mishap does occur, however, a sincere apology should come quickly and steps should immediately be taken to compensate for the damage (a big charitable contribution to a relevant cause, for example). Sometimes this isn't enough, however, and the

person involved must be let go – even when, in the case of Lululemon, it's the guy who started the business in the first place!

• Pitfall #5: Violating the Mission

For 31 years, Sharper Image sold high-end electronic gadgets designed to appeal to men with a lot of disposable income – and became a familiar sight in most of America's malls. But in 2002, *Consumer Reports* published a report that stated one of Sharper Image's air purifier products didn't do such a great job of purifying the air – as a matter of fact, the magazine said that the purifier released *unhealthy* levels of ozone into the space it occupied.

In other words, it did the exact opposite of what it was supposed to do.

Sharper Image tried to sue Consumer Reports for libel. The suit was dismissed, and soon the company was forced to accept massive amounts of returns on the product, including units that were many years old.

The merchant finally ended up filing for bankruptcy in 2008.

There is no bleaker scenario for a Mission-Driven company than to actually end up doing the opposite of what it sets out to do. JetBlue flirted with that scenario, but Sharper Image took it all the way by not only releasing an unhealthy healthy product, but defending it even when it shouldn't have. The resulting controversy not only cost the company millions of dollars in returns and lost sales, but also broke trust with the public.

How to Power Past this Pitfall

When something serious happens to derail your mission, you must take swift action and do whatever it takes to restore trust. That can mean doing things that seem to be insanely overboard – but it's better to do too much than what will be perceived to be too little by the public.

The corporation behind the pain reliever Tylenol wrote the book on dealing with this most difficult of situations way back in 1982, when several of their pills were tampered with on supermarket shelves in Chicago – and ended up killing seven people. As in the case of The Sharper Image, a product the public trusted to improve their health actually threatened it.

To deal with the situation, Johnson & Johnson, the Tylenol manufacturer, ended up recalling ALL Tylenol products from ALL across the nation at a cost of over $100 million. In the process, they saved a threatened brand and earned plaudits for their extensive action. As *The Washington Post* put it at the time, "Johnson & Johnson has effectively demonstrated how a major business ought to handle a disaster."[78]

When you do the opposite of what you promise, it threatens your very viability as an organization. Therefore, no action is too extreme to make things right again.

As you can see from what we've discussed in this chapter, a mission can be a very fragile commodity. But it doesn't have to be. If you remain true to your stated objectives and consistent in implementing them throughout your business practices, your mission should grow and thrive along with your profits. If, however, you ignore or take your mission for granted and fail to live up to its requirements, what could have been one of your greatest assets could end up to be your greatest weakness.

Our third and final section of this book is coming up next – and we have something special in store in it. In these final chapters of our book, we're going to profile four people who we believe are exemplary examples of what it means to be fully Mission-Driven, both in business and in life. You'll soon discover how each one of them fulfills their missions in very different ways – and their stories will in turn provide you with very different perspectives on how someone can bring put their missions into action both in their professional and personal lives.

You'll find out that these four people, however, do have one big thing in common; their ceaseless dedication to their causes.

---

78. Knight, Jerry. "Tylenol's Maker Shows How to Respond to Crisis," *The Washington Post*, October 11, 1982.

BOOK 3
MISSION MASTERS

*"The great and glorious masterpiece of man
is to know how to live to purpose."*

~ Michel de Montaigne

CHAPTER 12

THE NONPROFIT MISSION: BEN HOYER'S WAKE-UP CALL

Business: Downtown Credo Coffee Shops

Founder: Ben Hoyer

Location: Orlando, Florida

Mission: To improve the quality of life in cities by cultivating networks of meaning, impact and community.

Defining Quote: *"I made a decision from the beginning that money always follows the mission."*

You walk into a coffee shop. It doesn't seem much different than any other coffee shop, except maybe the people working there are friendlier than usual and seem to have a real bond with their regular customers.

You order something similar to your usual order at Starbucks, expecting to pay a similar kind of price for your coffee drink. But then you notice something radically out of the ordinary.

There's no cash register.

Then you notice something even more radically different.

There are no prices posted anywhere. Just "suggested" prices.

You look at the cashier in confusion. And he tells you, "You can pay whatever you think you should for the drink."

In a world where high-priced coffee drinks at national chains is a staple of late-night comedians' routines, this comes as the hugest shock of all. Pay whatever you want?

Is this any way to run a business?

Maybe it is – because Downtown Credo in Orlando, Florida, a nonprofit that we've been involved with for several years, has become such a success that it's expanding to more locations, despite the fact that founder Ben Hoyer never meant it to be a business in the first place.

I never really thought about it as running a business when I started it. I really thought about it as a nonprofit – as a matter of fact, we began by going to four local charities we respected and asking "What are you not doing that you'd like to be doing?" Then we tried to see if we could address those areas.

You can't get more mission-driven than Hoyer, a married father of two in his thirties, who has gained a lot of attention for this unusual approach to traditional business. As a result he's been profiled by various local, state and national media outlets, including *The Huffington Post*.

In these articles, he personally projects what he's all about – making the world a better place. One online blogger described their meeting this way: "You know those people you meet who just bring a smile to your face? Those people in your life you'd love to spend more time with because they make you feel so good about yourself and the world around you? That's Ben. He lives a life of purpose and meaning and by being around him you'll want to do the same."[79]

Hoyer grew up in Lake Mary, which is about 20 miles north of Orlando. He attended college at the University of Florida in Gainesville, Florida,

79. Brian Carlson Blog, "11 Questions with Ben Hoyer from Downtown Credo Coffeehouse in Orlando, FL," August 26, 2013 http://blog.briancarlsonphoto.com/2013/08/11-questions-with-ben-hoyer-from-downtown-credo-coffeehouse/

where he majored in religion. After living in St. Louis and Denver, he finally moved back to Orlando. He had been gone from the area for almost a decade and now had a family. He also had a mission.

I think the main thing was that, once I knew that I was going to be in Orlando long-term, I just wanted the city to be different. We bought a house and I knew I'd be here for 10 years at least. So I just started looking at how people serve cities. It felt like a lot of times when we serve cities, people who have stuff give some of it to people that don't have stuff. There's an implication there that your quality of life is tied to the stuff you have. I just don't think that's true. I think it's more tied to who we're becoming than what we have. I thought if I could lead with that idea, then it would gather a network of diverse people around that cause, and, eventually change the city.

When I started Downtown Credo, I was working at a church, where I was a little frustrated. In that role, I didn't feel like I was always able to fully be myself and I wasn't able to really engage with everyone in the city. My thought was Downtown Credo would allow me to work with all types of people and get them behind this cause.

Hoyer decided to plant his flag on an unlikely platform – coffee. He had read a lot about the coffee industry in college and knew it was a problematic business model. The people doing the hardest work, the growers, were getting paid the least. If he could address that inequity, he could demonstrate that one person could actually have a global impact – and he thought that was an important principle to illustrate.

We have this tendency to default to apathy – to say, "There's nothing I can do." To me, when we make that choice for apathy, we like ourselves a little bit less and we even enjoy life less. We'd all like to believe we can be people of impact.

Coffee was one place where I felt like things weren't as they ought to be – and I wanted people to realize how you can affect the way things are both locally and globally with the right small choices. I knew the concept of fair trade coffee was to pay growers a living wage – but I also knew that it wasn't really working and the growers weren't getting lifted out of poverty. Something more had to be done.

A friend of mine back in Gainesville who worked at a bagel shop spent time with coffee growers and paid them directly. I liked the idea and started selling his coffee one-on-one and a little online as well, demonstrating how you could treat people there fairly and have a significant impact. The idea mushroomed when I traveled with my friend down to Guatemala and was super-inspired. That's when the idea of the Downtown Credo coffee shop originated – as well as the idea of having customers name their own prices.

Hoyer joined his friend from Gainesville in paying the growers directly at 50 percent more than the fair-market value of the coffee. He then opened the coffee shop in the College Park neighborhood of Orlando, in a former yoga studio. He decorated the walls with art donated by local artists and built many of the shop's furnishings himself, with the help of friends – the rest came from thrift stores. At the time, he told The Orlando Sentinel, "Everything is homegrown and authentic to who we are."[80]

November of 2010 is when I opened – only weekday mornings, because I was just by myself and didn't have an espresso machine or anything. I closed down for the holidays and then, in January of 2011, we opened with full-time hours.

It was a little bit of a learning curve in terms of letting customers set their own prices. I told people the whole story of how I went to Guatemala and wanted to make sure the growers were fairly paid – and that, in turn, made a lot of people uncomfortable, as if I was trying to get them to pay $10 for a cup of coffee or something. The idea was to let them decide what they wanted to do – and part of that decision was realizing their potential to be a person of impact for good on the world.

We didn't have very many customers at first. We started very slow. But we just kept our expenses very low and added on as revenues increased. For instance, we only had half of a person on staff when we started - a part-time person and me, and that extra worker was only because I couldn't be there all the time. I was working another job at the time, so I didn't get paid at all, I just donated all my time at the beginning.

---

80. Newberry, Laura, "Downtown Credo: You pick the price at this Orlando coffee house," *The Orlando Sentinel*, March 12, 2012.

As Downtown Credo became more and more of a popular stop, Hoyer had to balance the growth of the business with the reality of his donation-only model, as well as the fact as he wasn't willing to ever take the place into debt. That meant he couldn't always afford what he needed to run the place.

The hardest part is staying committed to spending less money than is coming in. A big part of our growing pains is when we're using equipment that can't keep up with the traffic in the coffee shop – and have to commit to not buying new stuff until we have the money for it.

One time I got a call from the girl who was managing the shop. At the time, we had this really crappy espresso machine, but it was the one I could get from the "guy who knew a guy." It had already literally blown up twice. She called me that time because, now, it had caught on fire. She said, "There were flames inside of it - we need a new espresso machine" and I said "Sarah, what do you want me to do? You've seen the bank account. You know there's no money." She was angry, but once I told her how things were, she went ahead and fixed it and we kept on using it.

I also had no business training. I really believe the best way to work is to figure out quickly what you're good at - and only do that. While I was responsible for the books, we had a paper ledger in the drawer that totaled end-of-day and beginning-of-day cash. Before we bought supplies, I would check the bank account to make sure we had money. That was the level of accounting sophistication, because I'm a nonprofit guy not a business guy.

I would hire somebody that could put in an accounting system. I trusted them. Then when our operation outgrew their skills, they took a different job and I'd hire someone else with a higher level of sophistication. When I had to start filing forms with the IRS, I realized that was too crazy, and I hired a CPA. There's that learning curve at every point. We have QuickBooks, a payroll system, a tax accounting system, but I don't know how to do that stuff. I know how to ask just enough questions to keep people honest, but if I had to handle all that, it just wouldn't happen. Nothing else would get done.

Despite Hoyer's lack of business skill, Downtown Credo kept growing and now employs seven people as well as a full-time manager; Hoyer also works there full-time. And he's on the verge of opening two more coffee shops. Hoyer is able to afford that because most of the build-out costs are covered by others – and the stores are given very favorable lease terms primarily because its mission benefits other businesses.

What the coffee shop has done is attract the sort of person that people want at their places - a brand people want to be associated with. For example, a hospital is putting a Downtown Credo in the building that houses their executive headquarters. They really like us because they have a commitment to six different countries where they send medical equipment and medical teams to work with them. By putting Downtown Credo in a prime location, we can help tell the story of the work they do around the world. As a matter of fact, we're sourcing coffee from one of the countries in which they do work. That's why they're paying for the build-out where we're going to put the shop and also helping us buy the equipment - because it fronts a mission that they like. Rather than just putting another Starbucks in there, we are a direct representative of their mission. That mission alignment is what made the project work. They came to us and said "Hey, would you want to put a coffee shop down here?"

Our third location will be by a building that features co-working space for startups and such. That company came to us as well, because a lot of the demographics that might want to rent their co-working spaces are in our coffee shop already. Our coffee shop has become a meeting place for the demographic that works for themselves, those in their mid-20's to mid-30's. And that generation wants to align with brands that have more than one bottom line.

Of course, the very thing that differentiates Downtown Credo from other similar businesses – its emphasis of mission over by-the-numbers business practices – does sometimes cause some obstacles when it has to deal with the traditional business sector

For example, I can't tell you how much most people pay for our coffee. It averages out to the suggested amount. But I don't really know. They just slide it across the counter and baristas put it in a cash box. We don't track individual sales.

When I was doing the lease agreement for our new location, they let me structure the lease agreement. I wanted to tie our rate to revenue. If

we jump up in revenue in three months, we'll pay you more – but if that revenue goes down, we'll pay you less again. And they were okay with that. Then they asked the question, "How do you know what people are paying?" And I said, "I don't really know." They said, "Excuse me? That's not going to work. You're going to need to get a point of sale system." I replied, "Why, are you going to need a report of each individual transaction?" "No," was the answer, "but we're going to want the option to audit your daily totals to ensure you're reporting all the revenue."

I said requiring a point of sale system was a deal-breaker. "I'd love to work with you guys, but a point of sale system goes against what we're doing. If my baristas have to attach a dollar amount to every cup of coffee, it changes everything - because then they care about how much everyone is paying, and right now they don't." The thing is, we don't even give customers receipts. Our only record of revenue is how much cash is in the box at the end of the day.

In the end they agreed that the mission was more important than the narrowly defined tracking numbers.

Of course, they were sure we were getting ripped off. The lease guy said, "I guarantee people steal from you," and I told him, "If they are, it's not enough to cause a problem yet, so I'm fine with it. Once it starts causing a problem, we'll deal with it."

Downtown Credo has managed to triumph over the business-as-usual mentality because of its strong commitment to its own mission as well as specific social values. Hoyer always had it in mind that if he was firm in staying true to his principles, that commitment would translate into continuing growth and a lasting impact.

I made a decision from the beginning that money always follows the mission. If it's all about "How are we going to get more money to hire more people," it's not going to work. Instead, the shop has to be a place that builds community. The baristas make friends with the people that come in. And in addition to that, we facilitate other people meeting each other. We introduce them to each other. If you look at our Yelp reviews, many of them say, "You never know who you're going to run into at Downtown Credo." Customers met all these other interesting people and what that did is drove more traffic. More than word-of-mouth (and, by the way, we've never advertised), we rely on the efficacy of the mission: if we build community, people will want to be here. People want to live a life of impact and meaning.

There's one story that I really like. Chad, a programmer who coordinates a meet-up in town, started getting his group together in the coffee shop on Tuesdays. Over several weeks, we got to know him. Part of Credo's partnership is a neighborhood center in a low-income area, and I had been thinking it would be interesting to get these kids into the basics of computer coding. I asked Chad if he wanted to help, and he started going once a week to the center and teaching kids the basics of computer coding.

We were working on how best to teach that complex subject – and there was another guy that hung out at the shop a lot who was already teaching it to kids in elementary school and had developed a little curriculum. We beta-tested his curriculum for him in an after-school setting, and since then, he's adapted that curriculum and started a company. His program is now in six Orange County public schools and two after-school care centers.

As evident from that effort, Hoyer is taking Downtown Credo beyond coffee and into other diverse areas where he thinks he can make a difference. Below the words, "Refuse to Merely Exist" on the nonprofit's website, three specific missions are spelled out – Coffee, Rally and Conduit.

We're just continually trying to answer this question of, "How do we engage people?" We have these three divisions: Coffee, Rally, which is meant to tie in to four charities in Orlando, and Conduit, which so far has been introducing people to new skills. We're out to provide free skill-based workshops on a bi-monthly basis in things like photography, beer-brewing, songwriting, blogging, stuff like that. We're moving Conduit into a whole cross-discipline co-working base in a 40,000 sq. ft. area in a warehouse. I'm really excited to mix programmers, designers and filmmakers with small-scale financing and manufacturing – which will also facilitate internships with the kids we're working with.

In addition to the shop, we set up this social enterprise accelerator called Rally Makers, which helps new social enterprises start.

Organizations can apply for mentorship and money and we give them money in 5K increments up to 20k total, along with the mentorship. We've just completed the first round of that process and we're working on getting another round of donors to do it again.

Downtown Credo illustrates a few very important points about the power of being Mission-Driven. Here are three of the biggest takeaways that we'd like to point out:

If you build it, they will come

Downtown Credo began with virtually no capital and one worker (Hoyer) who could only work there weekday mornings. Because its mission was so strong and focused, however, it gradually built a strong customer base, grew its revenue and ended up expanding to two more locations.

The right mission attracts the right people

Part of Hoyer's mission was to give people a chance to come in and make an impact just by buying coffee – and many proved to be attracted to that kind of opportunity. Not only that, but they proved to be a desirable demographic for other companies in the city who wanted Downtown Credo to be a part of *their* mission as well. A higher quality of clientele grabbed the attention of higher quality businesses.

The mission should be placed front and center

By making the coffee a donation-only proposition, each barista was obligated to articulate Downtown Credo's mission in order to explain the unusual payment set-up. If it had been a traditional fixed-price system, that wouldn't have happened – and it wouldn't have stood out from the other coffee shops in the area. By ingraining the mission in the actual business operation, however, each and every customer couldn't help but hear what Downtown Credo was actually all about.

Ben Hoyer provides an excellent example of how a traditional nonprofit can make an impact by acting in nontraditional ways through creative engagement and outreach.

One of the Russian comic Yakov Smirnoff's most famous jokes about the old Communist regime was, "In Russia, you don't go to party.

Party comes to you." Well, the secret of Ben Hoyer's success can be found in that punchline. In other words, you don't go to Ben Hoyer... Ben Hoyer comes to you.

CHAPTER 13

THE MULTIPLYING MISSION: DR. BILL DORFMAN'S LAUNCHING PAD

Business: Century City Aesthetic Dentistry

Owner: Dr. William Dorfman

Location: Century City, California

Mission: To create a powerful brand that enables both other business ventures as well as charitable endeavors

Defining Quote: *"I didn't think outside the box. I didn't even know there was a box. I did things that nobody else did. For better or for worse, I just did them."*

Dr. William Dorfman is a reality TV star. A best-selling author. A wildly successful entrepreneur. A generous charitable contributor. A mentor to hundreds of kids.

And, oh yeah, he's a dentist.

Sometimes, a Mission-Driven business isn't about a specific purpose or mandate; sometimes it's just about the owner's proactive mindset and his determination to make the most of every opportunity that comes his way. As you're about to see, Dr. Dorfman always had a purpose to his actions, even as a young child – and, just as importantly, was always willing to go above and beyond what was required to fulfill his personal and professional missions.

That meant not simply building a successful dental practice that would serve his patients at the highest level - it meant *using* that practice as a launching pad to expand his personal brand into all forms of media, pursue entrepreneurial ventures and also provide mentorship and resources to those in need of them. In other words, Dorfman set and achieved *multiple* missions throughout his career that set him apart from the pack.

For example, he set his career path before he even hit Kindergarten.

The dentistry started when I was three years old. I was playing in the living room, when I fell and hit a coffee table so hard that, instead of knocking my baby teeth out, I actually intruded them back into their sockets. That meant I had to have multiple surgeries as a kid to ensure my permanent teeth would grow in without damage.

As a result, I became intrigued with dentistry. We had a great family dentist and I was just fascinated by everything he did to me. Where most kids would be horrified, I actually liked it – not the pain part, of course, but just analyzing how he was repairing the damage.

I don't know where that seed came from, but, from then on, I knew I was going to be a dentist. It never wavered. While most little kids wanted to be army men, I wanted to be the dentist that fixed the army men's teeth! And that actually made me feel really fortunate. Where a lot of my friends were really struggling with vocational options, I just had a clear path; if I wanted to be a dentist, I knew I just needed to do a certain sequence of things. It made growing up and going to college and everything so much easier – I wasn't all over the board, I was very directed.

Dr. Dorfman had a modest upbringing in the San Fernando Valley area of Los Angeles. He received his undergraduate degree from UCLA and was accepted to what he considers to be the best dental school in the country, the University of the Pacific (now known as Dugoni School of Dentistry) in San Francisco. When he graduated from their accelerated three-year program, he was ready to go to work – but not in the traditional kind of hometown practice most new dentists start out with. Instead, his Mission-Driven mindset led him to go for something much different.

Having grown up with limited resources, I never really got to travel or see the world. I thought, if I graduate dental school and immediately set up a practice, I'll never get to see anything. So I heard about a clinic in Switzerland that hired foreign dentists – it was the only one in the world where you could work with an American license.

They had 400 applicants for this one spot, and there was no reason they should hire me – I didn't speak French, I had no experience, I was fresh out of dental school, I was probably the least desirable candidate. But where I may lack in some areas, I don't lack in persistence and tenacity. I called that director of the clinic every week for months, and I had every professor at my dental school write me a letter of recommendation. When there were ones who were reticent to write one, I said "I'll write it, you just personalize it."

The clinic director got inundated with all of these letters, but I still felt like I wouldn't get hired for the position. So I asked if I could take him to lunch. He said "You're in San Francisco," and I said "Doesn't matter, I'll fly out." A bold statement to make when you have no money. I literally took out a loan from my grandmother to buy a ticket, and I flew to Switzerland, where he ended up hiring me. I got the job because I wasn't just a piece of paper like the other 399 candidates. Instead, I was a person right there in front of him who seemed capable and eager – so he said, "All right, I'll give you a chance."

I stayed in Lausanne, Switzerland for two years, and it was an amazing experience. I still have close friends from there. One honored me not only by asking me to be best man at his wedding, but also the godfather to his son.

In 1985, Dr. Dorfman returned to the Los Angeles area after his Switzerland stay and opened his own offices both in Century City and in the San Fernando Valley, where he had grown up. When the Century City practice took off, he closed the valley offices and focused his energies there. After working there for a while, he was approached by Stanley Vogel, who had been branded in *People* magazine as the

"Dentist to the Stars." Dorfman began helping out at Vogel's practice and the experience led to a significant turning point in his career.

I remember the first day I was in his offices, I saw Flip Wilson, Senator John Tunney and Linda Evans. I never met anybody like that growing up in the valley. What I ended up learning from Stanley was probably the most valuable lesson of all, and it wasn't about clinical dentistry – it was purely about how to talk to people, how to better communicate and how, especially, to deal with people in entertainment – this was a whole new breed to me.

I worked for Stanley for two years, and he gave me a very difficult case – I won't mention the person's name, but this was one of the most famous people in the music industry ever. He had a lot of dental problems, and I literally worked on this man for two years. I reconstructed his entire mouth with implants and crowns, and at the end of two years of treatment, on his last visit, Dr. Vogel walked in so he could see what I had done. Well, the man stood up from the dental chair, hugged Dr. Vogel and said "Stanley, thank you, thank you, thank you."

I'm like, "Hello?"

The man continued talking to Dr. Vogel. "Oh, your associate is good too, but Stanley, thank you." I'm sitting here, thinking to myself, "Stanley didn't do anything." At that point I decided, "I am going to open my own business."

At the time, I was dating a young woman who worked at Triad Artists, a talent agency which was later bought out by William Morris. She introduced me to all her friends who worked in the mailroom – many of whom became agency executives. They helped me build my practice by sending me their celebrity clients.

Again, Dorfman's ongoing mission was never going to be limited to his practice. In 1989, he started a company he named Discus Dental, and its first product was *The Smile Guide*, a book designed to help people see how their teeth – and their smiles – could be improved by cosmetic dentistry. But it was a chance encounter that really took Discus Dental to a whole new level of success the following year.

I've always been very philanthropic. I was working out in the gym, and a woman named Cynthia Hearn, who was kind of an accountant to the stars, approached me and said, "Would you like to help raise money for children's cancer research?" I said, "Absolutely." She said, "You're a dentist, right?" I said "Yes." "And single?" I said, "Yes... but...." I wasn't sure where this was going. "Well," she said, "we're doing a bachelor auction and we'd like you to go up on the block."

There ended up being 15 of us men up for auction by 850 women. They lined us up by age and I was the second-youngest one. The youngest one, the guy behind me, was someone named Robert Hayman. Robert was the son of Fred Hayman, who owned and developed Giorgio Cosmetics – so Robert had learned a lot about marketing and product development. Robert and I became best friends overnight.

In 1990, there was this proliferation of all these whitening products. I thought it was a good business to get into, so I approached Robert and we developed a product called NiteWhite. NiteWhite quickly became the number one take-home teeth whitening product in the country. We were competing with some really big companies in dentistry, but we were a lot more nimble – literally only two people in the decision-making process – so we could easily navigate through problems and quickly come up with solutions.

We did something that had never been done in dentistry. Cigarette companies had figured it out early – make smoking sexy. It may kill you, but you're going to look really sexy doing it. No one had used sex appeal in dentistry; we did. Instead of using our wife or our sister's best friend, we hired real models – like "whoa, really?" beautiful, beautiful models – and we shot them naked. You didn't see breasts, but we shot it very clean like a cosmetic ad. We also made it multi-ethnic – all of our ads looked like a Benetton Ad.

If you looked at all the whitening products prior to us, they looked like a medical mishmash. We packaged ours beautifully – it looked like an elegant cosmetic in a box. We also flavored it and did a few other things that nobody else did, and we priced it affordably. And we hired amazing sales reps.

The company started to grow and grow and grow. In the first year, we did $2 million in sales. The second year $4 million. Then $8 million, then $16 million. Then I went back to school. I knew how to be a *dentist, but I didn't know business – so I went to UCLA and I took night classes in business and accounting, things I needed to know so that when I sat in our board meetings, I could make a difference.*

Dr. Dorfman was determined to make a difference in other ways too – and the success of his NiteWhite product allowed him to make his first substantial foray into philanthropy. Greg Anderson, representing a group of dentists that called themselves the Crown Council which was dedicated to promoting oral health and doing charitable work in communities, approached Dorfman and his partner with a proposal.

They wanted to know if they could buy our whitening product at cost – one of their members, Dr. Jeff Gray from San Diego, had come up with an idea they called Smiles for Life. The idea was they would run a national ad campaign for patients to come and whiten their teeth at a reduced rate. But, instead of paying the dentist for the whitening treatment, they would be paying Smiles for Life, which would donate proceeds to children's charities.

When we heard what they were planning to do, we said that we'd give them the product for free. We donated all the whitening product, and to date they've raised over $35 million for children's charities. That was when we really started getting into a lot of philanthropic endeavors – for example, we also helped fund the Children's Dental Center of Greater Los Angeles, which provides quality oral health education and treatment services to needy kids and their caregivers. As our company grew, we gave millions and millions to these different charities.

Dr. Dorfman was anxious to continue growing as well as contributing – but sales at his Discus company sales had plateaued. It was hard to push past the $76 million mark, because Crest White Strips and numerous other whitening products were coming out and providing increased competition.

It was time to find a way to increase his public profile and potential. That way actually found him.

One of my patients had been a game show hostess for Howard Schultz, a TV producer who was trying to launch a new show on ABC called Extreme Makeover. In 2003, she had lunch with Howard and he told her about this show - she said "You need to meet my dentist." She also set him up with the plastic surgeon, Dr. Garth Fisher for the show – and Garth also said "You should meet my dentist." Of course, he was my patient too.

So I got a phone call from them asking if I would do the show. This was before reality TV had really taken off. I was a little reluctant, because I didn't know what I was getting into and how they were going to treat these patients. After I met with them, I really liked them – I felt like their hearts were in the right place. We went and we filmed the pilot for Extreme Makeover. It had huge numbers – ABC picked it up for the first season, I think 22 episodes.

Dr. Dorfman immediately saw the value of this kind of media exposure – and was willing to take a short-term loss in order to realize some substantial long-term gains.

Whereas Garth wanted to have a lot of other plastic surgeons on the show because he was afraid of being targeted, I didn't – I wanted to be the only dentist. My very first patient on the show needed 20 daVinci veneers – 10 upper and 10 lower – and at the time I was charging $1,500 per veneer. That added up to $30,000 worth of dental work.

Now, in the pilot, the three people I worked on just needed whitening treatments – so when ABC asked how much I needed to be compensated for them, I said, "Well, I'm an owner in the company, you don't need to pay me." But now, this time around, the cost was $30,000. Everybody on the show got paid – the hairstylist, the fashion people, everybody. So I sent them this invoice for $30,000 and they freaked out. They called me back and said, "Look, is there any way that you can just do three veneers?" I said, "No." That wouldn't have been fair to the person.

Then I made a deal with them. I said "I'll do all the dentistry on this show for free as long as I'm the only dentist and you give my laboratory credit for everything they do, because the lab bill is expensive. Also, I want to use the whitening product from my company." They said fine. I was virtually the only dentist on the show until it got so busy that I brought a few of my friends in to help.

Well, because of Extreme Makeover, our company just literally exploded. In that first year, 2004, our sales went from $76 million to

$101 million. Then we went to $135 million the next year. We had our biggest year in 2007 – the last year of the show – when we did $176 million in sales. ABC didn't pay me, but I did okay.

Knowing the company had reached maximum value, Dr. Dorfman and his partner knew it was time to sell the company – and finally in 2010, it was bought by Royal Philips Electronics, a firm based in the Netherlands that manufactures many health care products, including sonic toothbrushes. With the proceeds, Dorfman was anxious to take on his next mission – and this one would not be for profit.

The Crown Council had a boot camp program which was designed to teach skills dentists need to be successful in terms of running a practice from a business standpoint, nothing about clinical dentistry. Dentists would go through this program with their whole team and they'd say, "You know, I wish there was something like this for our kids." So the Crown Council founder created a mentorship program which was amazing – and they would call me in every year to talk with kids. I loved doing it.

Well, the Crown Council founder passed away at the age of 85 – and I really felt that left a void that needed to be filled. So I called his younger business partner, Steve Anderson, and Steve and I co-founded the nonprofit foundation LEAP, a motivational leadership program for high school and college students, aged 15-24. We teach kids skills they need to be successful in life, such as time management, money management, interviewing skills, and how to write a resume. We also teach them things like dating and eating etiquette, how to write appreciation notes and thank people. We do a whole segment on drinking and driving, and I do a program called "100 Year Lifestyle," where I basically say "At your age, if you take care of yourself and you eat well and you exercise, you should be healthy at 100." 60% of the kids come on scholarship and they are underprivileged. These are kids that come from families that could never afford to send them to a program like this, and they're brilliant kids.

What Dorfman and his partner provide is a concrete way to help their students attain the kind of Mission-Driven mindset that helped him succeed in so many different ventures.

One of the first things we do at LEAP, during the very first hour when the kids are sitting there waiting, I say, "When you woke up this morning, whether you thought you did it or didn't think you did it, you put a number on your head from one to ten, one being the lowest and ten being the highest. That's how you think about yourself. So how many of you put a ten on your head this morning?" All my kids that have already gone through my program know to put up their hands.

Then I ask, "How many of you didn't put a ten on your head?" The rest of the kids in the audience sheepishly raise their hands. I look at them and say, "Who picked the number? Did you have to take a test? Did you have to qualify in any way shape or form?" The kids shake their heads. I say, "You picked the number. If you don't think of yourself as a ten, no one else will. Wipe that number off and put a ten on there." And, throughout the week, we tell them to not only think like a ten, but to surround themselves with friends that are tens, to walk like a ten, to talk like a ten, that's a big thing. There's one kid, Scott, every night, he sends me a text, he says, "Dr. Bill, you're a ten million." That's great feedback to receive.

And we follow up. For example, Kyle Thomas. Kyle is a young man I've been mentoring for four years now. At 19, he was in a devastating automobile accident that left him a quadriplegic. He was drinking and driving. I trained Kyle and taught him how to be a public speaker. We take Kyle out to groups all over the country where he can speak to kids about drinking and driving. You or I can get in front of kids and say, "Don't drink and drive." When a kid paralyzed in a wheelchair says, "Drinking and driving is the stupidest thing I ever did my life," they listen.

There are kids that come into our program that have never been told by anyone that they are good at anything. They had no support structure, nothing, and now they are part of a community of kids that will care about them and listen to them. They've got friends, people that want to make them better and it's amazing what happens. It's unbelievable, I see it all the time. Parents will say, "What did you do?" Well, number one, I'm not their parent, that gives me a big advantage because you can't talk to your own kids the way someone else can talk to them. Number two, I bring in kids to talk to kids. That's powerful. I surround these kids with great mentors, leaders, and idealists. Birds of feather flock together.

I lecture to adults and dentists, but if you can help a kid, you can help them for 90 years. If you help an adult, you get the back nine - most people aren't going to reach their maximum potential in their 70's and 80's. With kids, it's this blank palette. I watch these kids grow up, I watch them become doctors and dentists, whatever it is they end up doing, and I take so much joy and pride in it.

Dr. Dorfman is now semi-retired from dentistry. Although his practice is still going strong, he only does dentistry about 20 hours a week. He's also still very much in the media mix, appearing in a new TLC show entitled *Smile*, and also producing his own series, *The Dr. Bill Show*, in which he follows up on people he mentors to see if they succeed in their paths.

There's no question that Dorfman was born with his Mission-Driven mindset. It's been his greatest gift and that's why he wants to pass it on to a whole new generation.

Since an early age, I knew I was different. I mean, for good or for bad, I knew I was different. I never conformed to what everybody else thought - I always thought for myself, whether it was popular or not popular. In first or second grade, I just looked around and thought, "These kids are immature"

I didn't think outside the box. I didn't even know there was a box. I did things that nobody else did. For better or for worse, I just did them.

I wake up every morning, I'm the happiest person you'll ever meet, I don't take anything for granted, I'm so appreciative of everything. My feeling is if we can't make this world better for having been here, what a waste. I've been so fortunate and anything I can do to make this world better or make other people's lives better, that's what I'm committed to. I don't do TV for fame, I think it helps get a better message out.

Eva Longoria is one of my patients and I love what she said; "The best thing about being a celebrity is that people will listen to you and you can do good things with it."

CHAPTER 14

THE GLOBAL MISSION: CHELSIE ANTOS AND THE POWER OF SISTERHOOD

Business: Trades of Hope

Co-Founder: Chelsie Antos

Mission: To help struggling women both here and abroad make a sustainable living and lift them out of poverty.

Defining Quote: *"My parents showed me that business can empower you, give you choices, give you freedom, and make you really believe in yourself. So I was passionate about helping other women do that too."*

You won't find many entrepreneurs who started at a younger age than Chelsie Antos.

It's rare that someone on the verge of turning seventeen is involved with getting a mission-based business off the ground. And it's rarer still to see that business flourish and thrive through an extensive worldwide network that provides women in developing countries with a path out of poverty – and women in America with an entrepreneurial opportunity.

But Chelsie was schooled in mission-based entrepreneurism at a very early age – you might say, from birth.

I had a background in business, my parents were pastors, but they were also entrepreneurs. They loved the model of business, they were passionate about how business could be used to change lives through pastoring.

That background came about because my Dad owned a very successful company that had been in my family for 50 years. We were an environmental business specializing in water reclamation and recycling technologies. He owned that business for most of our lives and, since I was home-schooled, I was able to go on field trips with him on his business trips once a week.

During these trips, we would spend time together and he would explain things to me, like how to deal with clients. I might be doing my math lessons while I was with him - and he would teach me how to relate that math in the real world, when you're doing business. My Mom was very involved in this family business and she also started different ministries and groups where she would work with women to empower them to become world-changers. Together, they also pastored a church. When I was 14, we took a business class that my Mom taught, and her first assignment was, we had to start our own business. So I started my own fitness training business. I had four different clients, which was a huge deal for me. Though they were probably helping me out because of how young I was, they were happy with their results and it was a cool process. And I ended up making enough money to buy a plane ticket to Italy for a school trip.

Because of my homeschooling, I was able to enroll in college early. That's when I began to see that my parents had ingrained this sense of entrepreneurship in me – and that business can empower you, give you choices, give you freedom, and make you really believe in yourself. So I was passionate about helping other women do that too.

That led her to join her mother, Holly Wehde, as well as another mother-daughter team, Gretchen and Elisabeth Huijskens, in founding a new company that would, in fact, provide a measure of hope to women all across the globe who face incredibly difficult economic circumstances on a day-to-day basis.

One of our partners, Gretchen, had started an orphanage in Haiti – which, of course, is so important and needed. But she began to not only look at the babies that were being brought into the orphanage – but the mothers who were bringing them in. These were women who had to give up their children because they simply didn't have the resources to take care of them. And she could see that there was a need for change at the root of the problem. If these moms could be empowered and given an opportunity to make an income, they could support themselves and their children instead of having to always rely on charity.

That was the seed of Trades of Hope. We were passionate about it, but you never know how you're going to get a dream to reality and it can be a hard transformation. So we used our own resources, built our own websites, innovated our own processes, and didn't take an income for the first two years. This was an amazing journey for me, because I had gained experience as a young teenager starting businesses - so it, in a way, helped prepare me to do all of this.

We began reaching out to artisans all over the world who could create and design products for us to sell. The idea was that these women in developing countries could make a steady income and we could bring these products to the U.S. market, and sell them through home parties. This is similar to the home party concept of Mary Kay, which sells beauty products in a woman's home. Our idea was to reach out to American women who wanted to be entrepreneurs themselves while also empowering artisans worldwide. They would take these products and become our army of marketers - we call them compassionate entrepreneurs. Basically, they bring our artisans' products to the American people, speaking for these women in developing countries and sharing their stories. They also make a percentage of whatever they sell, which creates the sustainability factor of Trades of Hope.

Meanwhile, we would make sure that our artisans were paid fairly. They now make approximately 3-6 times more than they would normally earn in their countries. They make 100% of the asking price for their products – and it isn't until after we have paid the artisans that we add on the final business costs and the percentage for the compassionate entrepreneur.

As Trades of Hope progressed, the founders had to forge viable connections with women artisans in undeveloped countries who could deliver marketable products to sell. They tapped into networks that would help them identify potential candidates.

At the beginning, we didn't have a ton of connections. We would research through mission groups and other organizations that were doing very reputable things all over the world. We worked with missionaries who were ministering to women both mentally and emotionally, but maybe weren't quite able to meet their economic needs – we were hoping to fill in that gap. And that's how we did it, working through all kinds of groups that could help us identify women to work with us. They helped point the way for us. They knew the need, they were living in the same country, and they could say, "Work with these women here."

There were also some artisan groups already up and running that didn't have an American marketplace to sell through. They might be trying to sell in their own country, online, but, outside of those borders, no one had ever heard of them before. They were selling to the poor in their own country and didn't have access to a wider market. We would be able to bridge that gap for them.

That's how it worked in the beginning. Now that we're bigger, most of the artisan groups contact us and then go through our application process. We look at it as an awesome opportunity to help them grow and to work with a wider audience – and, in turn, support themselves and their loved ones.

With the artisans in place, the next challenge for the Trades of Hope company was to find their circle of American compassionate eentrepreneurs who would be willing to help sell their products, which include jewelry, handbags, scarves, home furnishings and more.

Our compassionate eentrepreneurs began as our friends and family. They probably all thought we were little crazy, but we showed them our first sample kit and shared the compelling stories of these women all over the world.

As the people we knew became compassionate entrepreneurs, their friends also wanted to participate. We did do some marketing, but most of our recruiting was just done through word of mouth. We were very intent on reaching women who wanted to do something on the side that gives them purpose as well as extra income. Our excitement for Trades of Hope was contagious and that's how we signed on many of our compassionate entrepreneurs.

At this time, we have a website and multiple marketing campaigns – just, in general, more of a process in place - to find new consultants. Still, a lot of it is through word of mouth, which keeps us growing. We're currently up to about 1500 compassionate entrepreneurs right now, located all over the United States.

To get them started, they purchase a starter kit online at our website at www.tradesofhope.com. We have various kits, running from $69 (designed for college kids who want to sell out of their dorm) all the way to $399 (a kit that includes a wider selection of samples from our products and even a personalized website to use for marketing). Each kit contains some business supplies to get you started, as well as access to our online training resources.

You can then use the kit to go to a friend's house, set up a display, and share the stories of the artisans who craft these products. Whoever attends the party can then pick what products they like best and fill out an order form to purchase it. The compassionate entrepreneur goes back home and logs into our website's back-office system, place the orders and then the products ship right to the customers' homes. Our compassionate entrepreneurs can also host parties online and many do "Facebook" parties, which is another great option.

If you're not one of our compassionate entrepreneurs, you can still go ahead and host a "Home Party" or "E-party," through our website. When you contact us to host a party, we put you in touch with one of our compassionate entrepreneurs in your area, who will come share our products with your friends.

Chelsie has been gratified to see Trades of Hope succeed to such an amazing extent in such a short period of time. But she's also careful to make sure that she and the other founders don't lose touch with the enormous network they've created. To that end, she travels all across America to visit with their compassionate entrepreneurs and see first-hand how they follow through with their roles.

We're at this awesome point of growth and really feel like we're a sisterhood. That helps fuel the idea that our sisters are overseas and we're helping them as well. As we grow, we want to maintain that personal connection, that closeness that we're rooting for one another.

That's why I frequently travel the country to meet or catch up with our compassionate entrepreneurs. On the last trip, we had 31 different stops. We had meet-ups with all our compassionate entrepreneurs and I shared my personal story. I've been overseas multiple times and met many of the artisan women who provide us with great products. Telling their stories to our U.S. compassionate entrepreneurs helps fuel their passion and makes them even more motivated to sell for these women.

I love our compassionate entrepreneurs - it's cool to have 1500 people that are all united in the same purpose of ending poverty. Many of these women are stay-at-home moms – some also have other careers but they want to do something to change the world and end poverty, but they can't necessarily fly to Cambodia and live on the ground there. This is a way for them to actively make a difference in another woman's life and have a purpose that feeds their soul – all while making an income to help put food on their own table, send their kids to college, whatever financial need they might need to meet. They're passionate about Trades of Hope and that makes it exciting for us all to work together.

The artisans who provide products to Trades of Hope have overcome some incredibly traumatic incidents in their home countries. One of the most powerful stories centers around one woman who felt completely hopeless about her future – to the extent that she felt unable to even go out her front door any longer.

A woman in Cambodia named Chaya (name changed for artisan's safety) was the victim of what's called an acid attack. In many underdeveloped countries, there is this idea that one can shame someone by throwing acid on them, something that leads to the disfiguring of the body and face – and often the victim is simply a woman who decided to speak out for herself. The attack can even happen at the hands of someone in their family.

Chaya wrote to us about three years ago. She couldn't leave her home anymore, as she was often spit on, abused, and called awful names. In her community, they believe in reincarnation so they also believe that Chaya did something very evil in her past life to deserve this kind of humiliating treatment. It got to the point where even Chaya believed it. What went through her mind like a drumbeat was, "I'm worthless, I'm an animal, I deserve this." She couldn't ride on the bus to travel anywhere, so she stayed in the house and grew completely depressed.

She needed to sell things made from her home so she could make money and take care of herself. We were excited to help, so we sent her suggestions for things we thought she could make. As she started sending us products, she would ask "Is this a good idea? Do you like these colors?" We began to see her bloom. And she began to see herself as an artist.

Now, two years later, she's the head of an artisan group. She's excited she can help other women now, she doesn't just have to help herself. She flies to Thailand and Vietnam to get different products and the resources to get more. She views herself as a business woman, an artist and a designer and she feels wonderful about the fact that she can help other women like her.

It's the kind of movement that will change the face of poverty, because it's happening at the grassroots level right in these artisans' communities. We don't just want to come in and 'save the day' for these ladies, we want to provide an opportunity for them to save the day for themselves and their own families through empowerment.

Currently, Trades of Hope employs artisans in the countries of Bangladesh, Cambodia, Colombia, Costa Rica, Guatemala, Haiti, India, Jordan, Kenya, Nepal, Peru, Philippines, Thailand, Uganda, United States and Vietnam – with, no doubt, more locations on the way.

To further its mission, Trades of Hope also has in place a program it calls "Gifts of Hope," where, throughout the year, the business gives donations to programs that promote long-term business or education. The money for these donations comes right out of the profits from their product sales.

The future looks great for Trades of Hope – and for the women it employs in this country and others all over the world. By using a business model to accomplish its mission, it has gone beyond the limited impact of one-time charitable contributions, which are obviously important.

But it's more important to give these women an ongoing and viable way of making a living, so they are empowered to not only take care of themselves, but others in need in their communities.

We've more than doubled in size every year – and we're projecting tripling our growth this year, allowing us to make an even bigger dent in worldwide poverty. Last year alone, we employed 6,585 artisans all over the world.

Four years ago, this was just a dream. We were hoping we could accomplish something, but we didn't know how effective we could really be. But today, to reach the heights we're at is incredible.

We've been told that, when you help one woman out of poverty, she brings four other people with her. Our artisans are helping their children, aunts and uncles, parents, others in the community in need. And if that 1 to 4 formula holds up, that means we're impacting over 26,000 people.

We base how we treat our artisans on the principles of Fair Trade - where someone can make a fair wage and be empowered through their work and not just take hand-outs. They can know they've actually earned that income. They can know they have the ability, the smarts, and the skills to take care of themselves and that's huge to them. We want to continue doing that this year and just keep growing it for years to come.

Trades of Hope provides a unique and powerful template for others who want to create a Mission-Driven business that delivers these kinds of wide-reaching results – and Chelsie has some valuable advice for those who'd like to duplicate their success?

Think of it as a partnership. None of us can do it by ourselves. We needed to learn from other people, we needed to find mentors, not just in business, but also in nonprofits and in home party companies.

You need to be bold and call them or email them and say, "Will you mentor me?" And just ask them to pour into your life, because none of us started off knowing much about any of this.

When you have something you're passionate about, you can change the world - but you do need those people who have walked before you.

And you can't be afraid to ask them for help, because the only way you're going to get success is by asking for that help and seeking out those resources.

Trades of Hope is unique in our portraits of Mission-Driven organizations because of its innovative blend of business and altruism. The former feeds the latter, which is why Trades of Hope was not founded as a nonprofit. That very fact, in the founders' minds, strengthens their capabilities to do more and help more people. It motivates their compassionate entrepreneurs in America to sell as many products as possible – which, in turn, provides their artisans with a consistent and fair income that helps them pay for food, shelter and clothing.

Chelsie sums up the mission, as well as the company's method of fulfilling it, thusly:

We set up Trades of Hope as a business because we believe that model can be the mechanism of change. We love nonprofits, have friends that have nonprofits, but they serve different purposes. In the case of our artisans, charity will only get these women so far. We'd like to think compassion doesn't run out, but unfortunately it does. Here in the U.S., if you have trouble feeding your own kids, your compassion is going to run out. You're going to have to get a job. So why not allow the woman in the U.S. to make that income, while also helping her sister in a developing country to support herself? It's a sustainable cycle of change.

CHAPTER 15

THE TRANSFORMATIONAL MISSION: PETER DIAMANDIS' QUEST TO CHANGE THE WORLD

Occupations: Engineer, Physician, Best-Selling Author and Entrepreneur

Founder: XPRIZE Foundation, Students for the Exploration and Development of Space, Rocket Racing League

Co-Founder: Singularity University, Space Adventures Ltd., International Space University, Planetary Resources, Human Longevity Inc., Zero-Gravity Corporation

Mission: Passionate about innovation and creating a world of Abundance.

Defining Quote: *"The best way to predict the future is to create it yourself."*

Among the many, many honors he's received, Peter Diamandis was recently named one of Fortune magazine's "50 World's Greatest Leaders"[81] – and with good reason. Armed with an unshakeable belief

---

81. Fortune Editors, "The World's 50 Greatest Leaders," *Fortune*, March 20th, 2014

in his cause, Diamandis spearheaded private industry's entry into space exploration, despite a lack of significant money and resources.

As we related in Chapter 10, Diamandis has been nothing but Mission-Driven from a very early age and, as a result, has achieved amazing things – both through the many companies, schools and foundations he has created as well as through the powerful incentive competitions he has set into motion. His latest best-seller, *Bold: How to Go Big, Create Wealth and Impact the World* (co-written with Steven Cotler), offers specific advice on how anyone can put ideas into action the way he has.

The only problem with that advice? Diamandis is not just anyone. However, he remains an out-of-this-world role model for anyone passionate about pursuing a specific mission.

We've had the privilege of working with Peter on several projects, including producing a documentary, *Visioneer*, which showcases his many exciting ventures. We're also grateful for his attendance at several of our events, where he provided an incredible level of inspiration to the lucky clients who were there to hear him speak. Being around this charismatic visionary is always a treat – which is why, when it came time to put this book together, we knew Peter's unique voice and breakthrough thoughts needed to be a part of it. Fortunately, he was gracious enough to agree to talk with us for the purposes of this chapter.

In his own book, Peter discusses at length the importance of having an MTP (Massively Transformational Purpose) – which is the equivalent of being Mission-Driven in *our* book. We asked him to speak a little bit more about his own personal MTP and how it spurred him on:

I grew up inspired by the Apollo program and by Star Trek. My heart and soul really connected with that, and I feel very lucky to have had that inspiration. However, I grew up in a family that was very much a medical family and urged me to become a doctor. I remember one day telling my mom I wanted to be astronaut and her response was, "That's nice son, but I think you need to be a doctor." She said it in a very caring way, and I ended up pursuing medicine to make my family happy - but also, because I realized if I wasn't a fighter pilot, the next career that had the highest acceptance rate in the astronaut core was a physician. So I rationalized that and went that route.

But the passion of wanting to go into space never left me. When I went through MIT, when I went to Harvard Medical School, I got to meet a lot of astronauts, and I realized after some time that my chances of becoming one were relatively low because of the acceptance rate. Even if I did get accepted, did I really want a career as a government employee? I'd only get a chance to fly once or twice in my career, and I'd have do what I was told. That wasn't what I wanted for myself. I ended up channeling that frustration into building a series of entrepreneurial efforts in the space arena and, finally, starting the XPRIZE foundation.

For me, space was my guiding star, it inspired me, it woke me up in the morning, it ultimately drove me to start a dozen space companies. My mission and purpose in life has been to open the space frontier and make it accessible to humanity. I've added to that mission and purpose.

We've already related how Peter laid out a $10 million prize for the first entrepreneurs who could successfully launch a private aircraft into space. However, what we didn't do was fully detail everything he went through to make his XPRIZE come to fruition. His journey illustrates the necessity of truly believing in your mission – and doing whatever it takes to see it through – if you are going to achieve the success you're after.

He begins by discussing how he analyzed the incentive competition that motivated Charles Lindbergh to perform the first solo flight across the Atlantic, a contest that announced it would award the winner $25,000 – and realized how he could put the principles of that early 20th Century competition to work nearly a century later.

As I read Lindbergh's story, I made notes in the margin. I was amazed by how much money the teams were spending to win $25,000, some as much as $100,000. I remember totaling it up at the end, and being astonished that it was nearly $400,000 or 16 times the prize purse. Equally incredible was the fact that Lindbergh appeared to be the least qualified guy to win the competition given his short flying career at the time. I was fascinated by the idea that by offering up an incentive competition, a winner was automatically selected and financially rewarded.

I thought about that prize and its implications. A $25,000 purse, commanded $400,000 in team expenditures and ultimately gave birth to today's multi-hundred billion-dollar aviation industry. And, as I finished reading Lindbergh's book, I started thinking about a prize to promote spaceflight and wrote down in the margin, "XPRIZE???"

My thinking at the time was that perhaps a prize could be used to develop private spaceships for the rest of us. I had long since given up on the idea that I would actually travel to space as a government astronaut. But...if I could create a prize to encourage the creation of a new generation of private spaceships, perhaps that would be my ticket to space. Since I had no idea who would be my prize sponsor, I used "x" as a place holder, and thus the origin of the name XPRIZE.

A few months later I wrote up my XPRIZE idea. I then wrote an article that appeared in National Space Society magazine and was invited to give testimony in Congress about it. The year was 1994. It was during this testimony that I first met Doug King, who was about to become president of the St. Louis Science Center. One evening, over dinner, we started discussing the XPRIZE; Doug said, "You have to come to St. Louis. St. Louis is where you'll find the funds to support this vision".

Once the fourth largest city in the United States, St. Louis had descended to number 40, and was eager to regain its reputation as an aerospace leader. So, with my good friend and partner Gregg Maryniak, I traveled to St. Louis and met the one person that Doug believed could raise the capital, Alfred Kerth, who was one of the great thinkers and promoters of St. Louis. In my first meeting with him he got so excited he stood up and shouted: "I get it. I get it. Let's make this happen."

We met that evening at the Racquet Club for scotch and he laid out his vision. We would create the NEW Spirit of St. Louis organization that would follow in the footsteps of the original. The New Spirit of St. Louis (or NSSL) would be a group of 100 St. Louisans who contribute $25,000 each to provide the seed capital to launch XPRIZE.

On March 4th of 1996, we held another meeting at the Racquet Club, at the same table where Lindbergh himself had raised his original $20,000. That evening we raised about $500,000 from twenty St. Louisans who pledged to join NSSL. About two months later, on May 18th, we used *that seed funding to boldly announce the $10 million prize competition - albeit without actually having the $10 million in place!*

That day, hundreds of press outlets reported on the story and gave credibility to my idea. People got it; people believed it and it was a brilliant launch. But the hard work was just beginning - the work to fund not only the $10 million purse, but also the operation of the foundation itself. As bullish as I was, pitch after pitch failed to turn up a title sponsor. I presented to well over 150 CEOs, CMOs and philanthropists, everyone from Fred Smith of FedEx to Richard Branson of the Virgin Group, but the audacity of the prize and the chance that someone could die in the attempt, stalled our search for a sponsor.

The New Spirit of St. Louis Organization added members slowly $25,000 at a time and it was those funds that allowed us to continue operations.   These funds helped us continue along but ultimately were not enough to fund the purse. It was then that two friends of mine told me about the idea of a 'hole-in-one insurance policy', the notion that one could buy an insurance policy to underwrite the prize.

Here is the way it worked.

We had to set an end date to the competition. We selected December 31st, 2004. We would buy an insurance policy and pay a multimillion dollar premium. If someone were to win the prize by making the two flights to space within two weeks before that deadline, then the insurance policy would pay the ten million dollars. If no one pulled it off, then the insurance company would keep the premiums. We were basically placing a large Las Vegas bet.

Of course, the insurance company would also be betting that the efforts of Diamandis and his supporters would come to nothing – and that nobody would come knocking on their door to actually collect the $10 million prize. So the insurance company did the necessary legwork to assure themselves that no one would succeed at the XPRIZE mission.

The insurance underwriter hired a consultant to evaluate all the teams registered for the competition. They approached companies like Orbital Sciences, Lockheed and Boeing only to verify that they had no intention to compete. The big players were somewhat dismissive of the idea that a start-up entrepreneur could build a private spaceship and fly to space.

Luckily the insurance underwriter took the bet. All I had to do now was come up with a three million dollar premium payment. The problem was that I didn't have three million. What I did instead was negotiate with the insurance company a series of progressive payments. The XPRIZE foundation would make a $50,000 payment every month for a year, and then make a $2.6 million balloon payment at the end of that year. The insurance underwriter was effectively giving us runway to raise the funds. They didn't feel they had anything to lose - their expectation was that they would take our money and never have to pay anything out.

The first couple of $50,000 payments we made from funds we had raised. I made the next payment personally - and then we were out of money. Every month for the rest of that year-long period, Gregg and I would need to go and raise the money. It was not an easy task. I remember many Monday mornings knowing that I only had five days left to raise $50,000 or the competition was over.

Of course, the biggest challenge was being able to manage that $2.6 million due at the end of the year. If we had so much trouble raising $50,000, how would we manage an amount 52 times as large?

It was at this point that I met my guardian angel, who came to me in the form of a magazine article. I was in my Santa Monica apartment on a Saturday afternoon, catching up on some reading when I flipped through a copy of a Fortune *magazine issue featuring the "Wealthiest Women under 40." One of those women was named Anousheh Ansari and as I read her write-up, I stopped dead in my tracks. I read it over and over again in disbelief.*

"It is my dream to fly on a sub-orbital flight into space," Ms. Ansari was quoted as saying.

Yes, Anousheh, like me, had grown up watching Star Trek *and dreaming of becoming a space explorer. As I read further I learned that Anousheh, her husband Hamid, and brother-in-law Amir Ansari had just sold their third company called Telecom Technologies to Sonus Networks for over a billion dollars. That was when I knew I had found our sponsor.*

We flew down to Dallas to meet Anousheh, Hamid and Amir. We presented the XPRIZE vision and expressed our great desire to have them underwrite the purse and the operations of our first prize. According to Anousheh, they were sold within the first 10 minutes. I waited two days to hear from Hamid who called to say yes, that they would do it, that they would fund the operations and fund the remaining insurance payments. Shortly thereafter we announced the purse had been fully funded, and was now being re-named the Ansari XPRIZE, named in their honor.

Now, the only question was, could anybody win this before the December 31st, 2004 deadline?

Of course, there was still a major piece of red tape that Diamandis had to cut through – and the way he accomplished that impressive feat was surprisingly easy. But only because, once again, someone had responded to the power of his mission and wanted to be a part of helping it come to fruition.

In 2003, a year before the prize was to be awarded, in a meeting with Marion Blakey, the FAA administrator and Patti Smith the associate administrator I explained how the current FAA rules did not allow for private spaceflight. In order for the competition to be won in the U.S., the rules would have to changed, or teams would need to fly from outside U.S. territories. In her southern drawl the Administrator responded with, "Well then, we'll just have to change the rules, won't we?" True to her word she worked with Patti Smith to write regulations that ultimately allowed for private spaceflight to blossom.

The XPRIZE was to be collected only after two spaceflights had been accomplished – and the deadline was coming up fast. It wasn't until six months before the time would be up, on June 21st, 2004, that the first space flight was attempted. As it wasn't carrying a full load of three passengers, it didn't count as one of the actual flights required to win the prize, but it proved to be an invaluable and successful trial run.

The first official qualifying flight finally came three months later on September 29th – and the date for the second and final qualifying flight was set for October 4th, the anniversary of the USSR's launch of Sputnik, the first satellite ever to fly into space launched in 1957.

It's hard to fathom how much work went into reaching the October 4th, 2004 milestone. That day has been, and always will be, a special day for me. I remember leaving my Santa Monica apartment at 2:00 AM and driving 2 hours out to the Mojave Desert to meet up with my team. Through the night tens of thousands of people descended from around the world to be there for the historic event. With me that day were my mom and dad, my soon-to-be wife, Kristen and all of my closest friends. What I remember most vividly besides the ocean of people who had gathered, was the lineup of close to one hundred satellite news trucks camped out to watch and see whether Burt Rutan and Paul Allen could win the $10 million Ansari XPRIZE.

In the pre-dawn hours, the carrier airplane WhiteKnightOne was being fueled and SpaceShipOne was being readied. The pilot on this X2 flight was a Navy fighter pilot and SpaceShipOne test pilot Brian Binnie. Brian would go on to become our Charles Lindbergh. A tall, thin man with a generous attitude and a strong supporter of XPRIZE over the years, we could imagine no one better to carry the torch of commercial space on that day.

Just after sunrise, WhiteKnightOne's twin Williams FJ44 jet engines carried SpaceShipOne from the Earth's surface on an hour-long ascent to 60,000 feet. Our high-magnification TV cameras watched from the ground and broadcast the image to both the TV stations and large Jumbotron screens for the crowd to see. Edwards Air Force Base, a mere 50 miles away, watched the spaceship's flight on its radar, helping us measure its exact altitude to determine if we had a winner.

It was a magical moment when Brian's voice boomed out over the loudspeakers "Release, release, release". Seconds later SpaceShipOne was released from WhiteKnightOne, then a few seconds later its hybrid engine ignited and Brian was thrown back into his chair as multiple Gs hurled the ship upwards towards space. Brian flew a picture perfect flight. The vehicle not only exceeded the 100 kilometers required to win the $10 million but shattered the X15 altitude record set some 40 years earlier.

The winning of the XPRIZE was, of course, a pivotal point both in the advancement of Diamandis' mission as well as its ultimate expansion. The event ended up bringing many important and influential people into his orbit, people who were energized by his ambitions and, even more importantly, his ability to transform those ambitions into reality.

Another vivid October 4ᵗʰ memory was having the XPRIZE capture the coveted Google Doodle real estate. On the Google homepage, soon after the winning flight was completed, was an image of SpaceShipOne flying over the Google logo, next to it a small flying saucer with two green aliens observing the flight. That Google Doodle later lead to my addressing a room full of 4,000 Googlers at the Googleplex on the Ansari XPRIZE, and a subsequent lunch with Larry Page, Google co-founder (then co-President and now CEO). During that lunch I presented an impromptu invitation for him to join the XPRIZE Board of Trustees (which he happily accepted). His participation, along with Sergey Brin, Eric Schmidt, Wendy Schmidt, Elon Musk, Jim Gianopulos, Arianna Huffington, James Cameron and other notable figures who subsequently joined the XPRIZE Board of Trustees breathed new life (and capital) into XPRIZE, fueling our commitment to use prizes to take on the world's grand challenges and create large-scale incentive competitions where market failures existed.

What motivates these kinds of prominent business leaders and influencers to work with Diamandis and join in his mission? He sums it up in one word.

Passion. I think having my true passion shine through when I'm on the stage, or when I'm communicating, brings people to me. It's about speaking from my heart. It's being authentic in what I truly believe and having that come through. Whenever I don't...it fails. Whenever I do, people gravitate towards it.

It's that we have common aspirations, passions and interests to do big things in life. Google co-founder Larry Page once said something to the effect of, "I have a simple metric, a question I use now that says, "Are you working on something that can change the world, yes or no?" It's the experience of most successful people in the world that, when you revolutionize one industry, you're not satisfied ever again with incremental change, you're looking to do big and bold things in life. So you're attracted to people who do equally big and bold things.

Much of my work requires heavy financial backing – but there's a lot of wealth in the world. That's because there are a lot of people who've been successful, who have maybe learned to sell a widget better than anybody else to somebody else. And, a lot of times, my job is to help these people to go from success to significance, to help them see the bigger opportunity. These are the kind of people I tend to attract and work with. My goal is to work with them, partner with them, to go and create impact. There's plenty of capital out there. If you're not attracting the capital, it's because you haven't done enough work to make people take you seriously, or you're not communicating what you want to do properly. As I discuss at length in my book, you need to learn how to stage your effort and bring a community of people along with you to watch your successes and to allow you to go to the next one and the next one.

As Diamandis said earlier, his initial space mission has led him to embrace other important pursuits in which technology has the potential to solve pressing world problems. The more he can do to make that happen, the more he *will* do.

My mission has been to take my childhood, really, into most of my life. My forties were focused on spaceflight, and it was this epic mission that was very difficult, capital-intensive, time-intensive, and technology-intensive, and it culminated with the XPRIZE. As I teach people it's really important early in your career to have a real focus, something that becomes the centerpiece of what you're aiming at.

It was only after I had some success with space that I expanded my mission beyond that. I went into a larger orbit, if you would, beyond just the grand challenge of space and into even bigger challenges. If you can take on private space flight, you can take on a lot of other seemingly-impossible goals. I don't think it's the case that you have to have only one mission in your life, I think it's important to have something that you build on and grow with.

We are entering a point in history where entrepreneurs are now capable of doing what only the largest companies and governments could do before. Forty years ago, only a government could build a spaceship. Today, a small team of 30 engineers powered by exponential technologies can do it. In the same way I believe that there is no problem that cannot be solved, that entrepreneurs powered by technology can take on any challenge and find a solution, I believe that we've entered a day and age where we can stop complaining about problems and start solving them. That's how you can impact the lives of a billion people.

But finding that initial MTP (Massively Transformational Purpose) is something that I think is ultimately one of the most important first steps any entrepreneur, any CEO needs to take on. Whenever I talk to people now, I say, "Do you know what you would do in life if you didn't have to work, if you had all the time and energy and resources in the world? Do you have a mission, do you have a purpose in life?" That's one of the most fundamentally important things.

Peter Diamandis doesn't just talk about thinking big and doing big things – he actually finds the ways to turn intangible ideals into reality. By kick starting the movement towards private entrepreneurs taking on mankind's biggest challenges, he's opened up many more potential pathways to progress than have ever existed before.

There are very few missions of the magnitude that Diamandis has taken on in his unique and striking career. That's because there are very few individuals who are as Mission-Driven as he is.

AFTERWORD

NOW, IT'S
YOUR TURN

*"A small body of determined spirits fired by an unquenchable
faith in their mission can alter the course of history."*

~ Mahatma Gandhi

Missions excite people.

Whether it's the *Star Trek* crew exploring the universe on their five-
year mission or Tom Cruise taking on an impossible one, missions
make audiences the world over cheer for the hero who succeeds in
completing a difficult and daring one.

When you commit to making your organization a Mission-Driven
one, you have the potential to become that kind of hero - the kind
of hero people see as inspiring, exciting and transformational. You
have the potential to change your customers into fervent fans of both
you and your business, fans who will not only remain loyal to you
and supportive of your efforts, but who will also enthusiastically rally
others to your side. And you also have the potential to not only build
an explosively successful organization, but also to leave the world a
little bit better place.

In the preceding pages, we've hopefully given you all the basic tools
you need to create your own Mission-Driven company. We've shared
with you the secrets of why Mission-Driven businesses flourish over
the competition, how they spark stronger employee bonds, how they
bolster branding and marketing efforts, and how they create genuine

change not only in the marketplace, but in society at large. We've also provided Action Guides that can help you determine your own Mission-Driven destiny and we've profiled a few Mission-Driven pioneers who have put it all on the line to follow their inner passions. We've done all this because we believe in the Mission-Driven Business™ model – and we know that it delivers many powerful advantages that can't be obtained through conventional company practices.

And yet, Mission-Driven companies can also be extremely fragile. If they are seen to be hypocritical in not practicing what they preach, or, worse, actively acting against the principles of the mission they espouse, the public can turn on them on a dime. Being Mission-Driven is a two-edged sword; the very thing that makes you stand out can also bring you down if you're not faithful to its precepts.

That's why you can never be cynical about your mission – or take it for granted. If anything, you must believe in it much more strongly than the public does.

We hope you're as excited about the possibilities of being Mission-Driven as we are – and that, now that you thoroughly understand everything that's involved with this unique business approach, you'll put it all into practice and one day achieve the completion of your own personal "Moon Shot."

Even then, that probably won't be the end. We think you'll find the journey is the most rewarding part of the process – and that you'll feel a little twinge of disappointment if you are fortunate enough to achieve your biggest dream.

But that's okay.

That's when it will be time to set a brand new Moon Shot. And start all over again.

We wish you the best in all your Mission-Driven endeavors – and we thank you for taking the time to read this book. Good luck from all of us in Mission Control – and please contact us if we can be of any help to you along the way!